"I'm a bride weeks."

Violet threw the invite on the desk. "I RSVP'd with a plus-one and have never canceled it. And I really don't want to go alone. Don't suppose you want to pretend to be my boyfriend for a weekend in Florida?"

"Oh, I am absolutely down for that. What part of Florida?"

Violet opened her mouth but no words came out. She wasn't sure what was more shocking—that she'd made such an offer...or that Beck had jumped at it!

"The wedding is in Miami." Nope. Those were not the words that were supposed to come out. Shutting this down should be her goal. But Beck was hot. He would turn heads. But more importantly, he was kind.

If her ex pulled anything, and knowing him, he absolutely would, Beck would have her back. Fake date or not. On his arm, this wedding had a chance to actually be fun.

Dear Reader,

If I have a rough day, my furry coauthors can always make me smile. Like my heroine in *Fake Dating the Vet*, I own a pittie that loves to wear clothes. Actually, I own two! And Bucky loves to watch the athletically inclined pups at the dog park run through the agility course—watch, not participate. Watching those pups gave me the idea for a vet book with agility competitions in the background, and Beck and Violet's happily-ever-after was born.

Dr. Violet Lockwood grew up wanting the fairy-tale relationship her parents didn't have. She thought she had it—only to get left at the altar. Inviting Beck to be her fake date to her best friend's wedding was supposed to be a joke. But she can't say she is upset when the adventurer jumps at the chance!

Vet tech Beck Forester was a late-in-life baby, the apple of his parents' eyes and incredibly sheltered. As an adult he craves adventures. So when Violet offers him the chance to play out a made-for-TV scenario as her fake boyfriend, he can't say yes fast enough. There is only one rule to this fake fling—he is never getting married.

Juliette Hyland

FAKE DATING
THE VET

JULIETTE HYLAND

MEDICAL ROMANCE

Harlequin®
MEDICAL ROMANCE

Recycling programs for this product may not exist in your area.

ISBN-13: 978-1-335-94267-8

Fake Dating the Vet

Harlequin Enterprises ULC
22 Adelaide St. West, 41st Floor
Toronto, Ontario M5H 4E3, Canada
www.Harlequin.com

Printed in U.S.A.

Juliette Hyland began crafting heroes and heroines in high school. She lives in Ohio with her Prince Charming, who has patiently listened to many rants regarding characters failing to follow the outline. When not working on fun and flirty happily-ever-afters, Juliette can be found spending time with her beautiful daughters, giant dogs or sewing uneven stitches with her sewing machine.

Books by Juliette Hyland

Harlequin Medical Romance

Alaska Emergency Docs

One Night Baby with Her Best Friend

Boston Christmas Miracles

A Puppy on the 34th Ward

Hope Hospital Surgeons

Dating His Irresistible Rival
Her Secret Baby Confession

Redeeming Her Hot-Shot Vet
Tempted by Her Royal Best Friend

Harlequin Romance

Royals in the Headlines

How to Win a Prince
How to Tame a King

Visit the Author Profile page
at Harlequin.com for more titles.

For my spicy kitty, Groot. Without his constant
"snuggles" on top of my laptop, this book
might have been turned in on time!

CHAPTER ONE

THE PRISTINE WHITE paper with black and white flowers stood out on Dr. Violet Lockwood's desk. Fiona's wedding invitation had arrived almost five months ago. And she'd sent along her RSVP and plus-one four months ago.

It was the plus-one causing her issues now. Why hadn't she just marked that she would attend alone? Violet pinched her eyes closed and took a deep breath. She knew exactly why…because Thomas would be there.

With his new wife.

The one who looked just like her according to the texts she'd gotten when they started dating. His date was the woman he'd actually met at the altar.

If she'd RSVP'd honestly, she'd have had four months to get used to the stares she knew would come her way. Four months to practice her smile among the friend group she'd been so close to in college. Four months to find self-deprecating jokes about how the woman who'd craved a partner was stranded in perpetual singlehood in Maine.

Four months to ready her armor for Thomas's barbs.

Hell, she could have been truthful when Fiona asked her about her date a month ago—owned up to the lie no matter how embarrassing the whole thing was. She could even have lied, said that the relationship just hadn't worked out.

But no. Those were not the sensible paths she'd chosen. Violet had bragged about how hot the mythical man was, how good he was in bed, how excited she was for everyone to meet him. All without ever giving away a name. A ploy Fiona had been too kind to call her bluff on.

Now she was two weeks away, with the plate of chicken she'd ordered for the imaginary date. She'd meant to call Fiona and tell her to cancel it weeks ago. Own up to her failure.

She could still make that call. At least that way the servers wouldn't ask if anyone was coming to the empty place beside her. Violet had used up every excuse in the book. Even now the invitation was on her desk so the excuse of getting home too late to call after working as the on-call emergency vet vanished.

That was her plan a week ago when she'd dumped it in her backpack and sworn for the twentieth time that today was the day she gathered her courage.

She looked at the clock, seven o'clock. She still had almost four hours left on her shift, but no patients at the moment.

Violet let out a breath, but she didn't reach for her phone. *Coward.*

"You stare any harder at that piece of paper, it might burst into flames. If it does, I want to video it. I mean how often does that happen?"

"Never, Beck. That *never* happens." Violet rolled her eyes at the vet tech who was hotter than any man had a right to be. And, at twenty-six, ten years her junior, Beck Forester was so not in her dating pool.

That didn't stop her subconscious from filling her dreams with illicit things.

The man was just over six foot, with broad shoulders and the ability to dead lift an injured 110-pound Great Dane. And yet somehow he managed to sneak up on everyone in the clinic where she was a staff veterinarian.

He also blew through his annual vacation as fast as he earned it, jetting to far-off places whenever the whim set in. Two months ago, his hike through part of the Appalachian Trail was interrupted by a far too close call with a cougar. The man had stories that could keep you entertained for days.

"Never is a long time. It *could* happen." He winked, then pointed to the invitation. "What has you so cross about a wedding invitation, Doc?"

What indeed?

She laid the invitation down. "Think every wedding invite looks the same so it's obvious to nosy vet techs what someone is looking at even without reading it?"

"Maybe." Beck shrugged, not a care in the world. In the nearly two years they'd worked together, she'd never seen the man worry. Never watched a frown cross his lips. No pinched eyebrows or terse words to indicate he was having a bad day.

Nope. Beck always had a smile and was ready for whatever adventure came his way that day. The man was the definition of go with the flow.

Once upon a time she'd been good at that, too. A chance to go to overseas for an agility competition—yes please! Girls' trip just because—of course.

That was a lifetime ago and a very different Violet.

"That invite has been on your desk all week, right by a notepad that says 'call Fiona.' I saw it when I was grabbing Maverick's file, and then again when I came looking for Jack's. Sooner or later Dr. Brown is going to have to drop the paper system. And then the supplier will go out of business as I think he may be keeping them in the black all on his own."

He was giving her an out. A way to discuss something else. It was kind. And the topic of overflowing paper files was one every member of the office, except Dr. Brown, chatted about regularly—even though they all knew the answer.

The office would get a new system when Dr. Brown finally sold it. Probably to one of the corporate companies that came by every few months offering very generous buyouts. So far, Dr. Brown said he had no interest, but eventually the dollar signs would be enough.

Everyone had a price.

"I am a bridesmaid in a wedding in less than two weeks." Violet threw the invite on the desk. "I RSVP'd with a plus-one and never canceled the date. I hate the idea of going alone. Want to pretend to be my boyfriend for a weekend in Florida?"

"Oh, I am absolutely down for that. What part of Florida?" Beck looked seriously excited. For a moment she thought he might clap.

Violet opened her mouth but no words came out. She wasn't sure what was more shocking. That she'd made such an offer or that she ached to leap at the option too.

Beck jumping wasn't surprising at all. This was the kind of thing he lived for. He'd make the perfect date.

"The wedding is in Miami." Nope. Those were not the words that were supposed to come out. Shutting this down should be her goal. But Beck was hot. He would turn heads. But more importantly, he was kind.

If Thomas pulled anything, and knowing her ex he absolutely would, Beck would have her back. Fake date or not, on his arm this wedding had a chance to actually be fun.

"Cool. I have never been to Miami. How long have we been 'dating' for this ruse?" Beck made air quotes around the word *dating*.

"Beck." This was rapidly spinning out of control. He was excited, and for the first time in months she wasn't dreading what should be a happy occasion.

"I can't ask you to do this." Though in her head she was already plotting how to get him on the plane with her. She had a ticket…but he would need one too.

And with only two weeks to go, ticket prices would be astronomical.

"You already did." Beck grinned showing off the deep dimples in both cheeks. Of course the Adonis had dual dimples. That was another thing her brain insisted on imputing into her dream life. "Now I just need the details."

This was fully out of control. As great as it would be to walk into the wedding on Beck's arm, she couldn't do this. Shouldn't do it. She didn't need a man. She was thirty-six. She was a veterinarian. Her life was boring but it was hers. Her terms. Period. "Beck—"

"Violet." He mimicked her tone as he inter-rupted her. "I have a ton of mileage points, so my ticket will be free. I assume you already have a hotel room. I'll go halfsy with you on it, if I can sleep on the pullout couch. Do I need my tux for this or will a suit work?"

He clapped. The hot, twenty-six-year-old Adonis actually clapped at the idea of attending a wedding with her. "Or is it a beach wedding and I get to wear a swimsuit? I draw the line at a nude wedding." Beck put his finger on his chin, closing his eyes. "I mean maybe for the experi-ence I could go to a nude wedding…"

"No! No." Violet blinked as the wall of words and the image of a nude Beck on the beach gripped her brain. "No, it's black tie. Why do you have a tux?" Any question would work to try to get the spicy thoughts from her mind.

Beck chuckled as he moved; his tall frame slid-ing into the tiny office chair with such ease. "For occasions like this." He held up a hand, clearly anticipating a sharp retort.

"I'm not joking. For occasions like this. I found one at a thrift store in Texas on a trip a few years ago. Got it for less than twenty dollars and had it tailored. Now, I have it for a wedding date in Miami. The world is full of opportunity if you are willing to jump at it."

Right. That had been her motto once, too. That Violet had traveled the world, jumped at anything that sounded like fun. Fallen in love fast—and been devastated by the results. Lost her entire life in the process.

She'd rebuilt, but she wasn't the same person. One did not get to go back to the person one was after coming home to find the place practically cleaned out—after getting stood up at the altar.

"So it's black tie. We leave next Friday?"

"Yeah, on the first flight out. The rehearsal dinner is at six. I have handled all my bridesmaid duties long distance. Luckily, Fiona is the exact opposite of a bridezilla." Surely she wasn't actually going to do this. It was too much.

"Beck—"

"You on this five-thirty flight out? A layover in DC and then onto Miami?"

"Yes, but…"

"Cool. Booked. No backing out now, Violet. My points are nonrefundable. But I will warn you I am not a morning person. There is a reason I work the late shift." He held up his phone and playfully raised his eyebrows.

"Considering we will basically go from our shift to the airport, I won't hold it against you." This was happening. Really happening.

A fake wedding date. This should be a new low. But the twinge of excitement in her belly refused to accept any shame.

"So, what roles are we playing? I assume this is to get back at an ex."

Beck rubbed his hands together, and she couldn't help but laugh. "Why are you so into this?"

"Come on, Violet. How often do you get to pretend to be dating someone? It's like our own television drama. I am not missing out on this. So again, who are impressing?"

"You will impress everyone who sees you." Violet put her hand over her mouth, heat flooding her cheeks as Beck leaned a little closer. Damn the man was hot. And he knew it.

He cocked his head, those dimples appearing as he stared at her.

"My ex-fiancé." Violet rolled her eyes. "He left me at the altar…via text. An hour before we were supposed to say I do. He and his new wife will be there. It's dumb, but I don't want to deal with questions and pitying looks."

"Why go at all? Surely your friend will understand."

"Because Fiona and I were college roommates. She was my maid of honor, she passed me tissue after tissue while I cried over the lout who didn't show. Unfortunately, her soon-to-be husband is stepbrothers with Thomas. The two of them aren't close, but he doesn't want to upset their father. The man is getting on in years."

Violet blew out a breath. "Besides, it will be fun to see my old girlfriends. I am the only one who left the area." Fled was the actual term, but she was already dumping too much info on him.

She'd sold her and Thomas's condo, a task made infinitely easier by the fact that the only thing he'd left her was the unopened wedding gifts, her bed and clothes.

Thomas had even taken her grandmother's cross-stitched tablecloth. He'd played dumb when she'd asked for it back. He said he didn't have it. That Violet must have misplaced it. Like she'd lose the one family item she cared about.

His mother had posted a picture of it last Christmas that a mutual friend had liked so it made it across her social media. So Thomas had it—and was using it.

The ass.

With little to her name, she'd accepted the job from Dr. Brown and rebuilt her life in Bangor. On her terms. And she was not letting a man mess with her peace again.

"I guess not inviting your ex would make future family get-togethers awkward." Beck delivered the line without bothering to hide the fact he disagreed with the decision.

Neither Fiona nor her lovely fiancé, Patrick, were happy with Thomas's attendance, but it made Patrick's dad happy. Sometimes you did what you could for family.

"So, we have been dating at least six months? Or do we go for a year? We could be engaged. Oh, what if I am a billionaire tycoon? Secret prince of some foreign island?"

Violet laughed. The small chuckle broke free into a raucous giggle, and she hugged her belly.

Beck's chuckle mixed with hers. A deep baritone that made her toes curl. Dear God, the man was positively delicious.

"I think you, on your own, Beck, are more than enough to get the tongues wagging. Plus all of the stories of your trips will make for dinner conversation." Heat spread across her body, into places she didn't think it should, as she leaned closer to him.

"Great. Six-month relationship that we are just now taking public because of your less than grand dating history. But I made you put down the plus-one so I could prove I would still be there for the wedding." He raised his brows as he created the perfect story for why she hadn't included his name.

Fiona might even buy it.

"Thank you." She bit her lip as emotions crept up her chest. This was the nicest thing anyone had ever done for her.

"Any time, Vi."

Vi. Only he shortened her name. It was something he'd done once about a year after he'd started at the clinic. The receptionist, Lacey, had quickly corrected him. No one called her anything but Violet, or Dr. Lockwood.

Her mother had hated nicknames and refused to call her anything but her full name. Control was her mother's coping mechanism in the world. Its impact on others was never her concern.

She'd gone by Vi in college—until she met Thomas.

Thomas had made a face the first time he heard it used. He said she was as delicate as a flower; one did not cut a flower short. By the end of their relationship, his focus on her beauty irked her, but in that moment, she'd thought he meant well.

Professionally she'd chosen the full name. Something she sometimes regretted.

Hearing Vi from Beck's lips always brought out a grin. Which was why she never asked him to stop and why she suspected he kept doing it.

"So, do we pass the slow evening talking about the wedding, or backstory, or gossip from your college years to make sure we seem like a long-term couple?"

"Uh." Right, there was more to this than just showing up on a hot guy's arm.

The front doorbell chimed and Violet held up her hands. "None of the above it seems. You jinxed us."

There was no way for Beck to kick himself without Vi noticing. He'd been an emergency vet tech for nearly three years now, two in this clinic. He knew better than to mention the words *slow*, *quiet*, *tame*, *easy*. It was like asking for a rushed case.

And he'd finally gotten an invitation to see her outside the office. Playing her fake boyfriend would be the easiest game he'd ever had. The woman was brilliant. Funny. And drop-dead gorgeous. She must have men, and women, banging down her door to get a date but she refused to answer the knock.

He'd had a crush on her since the second night they'd worked together. A giant Great Dane had come in after eating one of his little human's socks, a surprisingly common occurrence. The mom was panicking because she'd forgotten to pick up the toddler's sock. The toddler was in tears because puppy was sick. The dad was worried about everyone and the vet bill.

Vi had sat on the floor, rubbing the giant dog's head while she outlined all the options. When the father quietly explained that they didn't have money if emergency surgery was needed, she'd told him, without judgment, that most of the time they could use other options.

The father had returned two days later—alone—tears streaming down his face because the dog was worse. He'd come to request euthanasia. Violet had explained that a donor had stopped in to pay for care for any family that couldn't afford it.

The relief on the patient's face as he took his

sleepy dog back home following surgery was seared in Beck's mind. As was the knowledge that there'd been no outside donor. Vi had done the surgery for free and taken the hit on the cost from her paycheck.

It was the first time he'd seen her act as the "mystery donor" but not the last.

Stepping into the reception area he was stunned to see Maria Miller and her border collie, Baby.

"Beck." Maria was on her feet, stress etched into the corners of her eyes.

"What is going on with Baby?" The border collie was basically Maria's child. The four-year-old pup was a champion agility dog. In fact, Baby was supposed to compete tomorrow at their local club. Though compete was little bit of an overstatement for tomorrow.

The gym hosted the monthly competition for fun, and more than one person came just for the potluck after.

"We were doing one more prep run; you know she loves them." Maria wiped a tear from her eye.

He could already see the blame taking over. "I know. This isn't your fault."

Baby, like most border collies, was highly driven. A breed bred to work, she was constantly on the go. He had his own border collie mix, Toaster. No matter how late he got home, he and Toaster would go through the agility course he'd set up in the back of the cottage he'd inherited from his parents.

"She let out a yelp as she ran down the A-frame. She tried to keep going." Maria buried her head in Baby's fur and let out a sob.

"The good news is she is walking. Let's get her into a room so Dr. Lockwood can take a look at her." Maria stood, holding on to Baby's leash, and followed Beck into the exam room.

He took Baby's vitals, then offered Maria a smile. "Baby is our only patient right now, so Dr. Lockwood should be in quickly." In the ER, patient arrival time didn't matter. It was worst-case scenario first.

He stepped out and found Violet waiting right by the door. Beck gave her the details quickly. She nodded, made a soft sound, then headed into the room. He followed.

"Did you run down the A-frame poorly, Ms. Baby?" Violet ran her fingers over the dog's head, scratching behind both ears. It was a nice petting for the dog, but he could see her monitoring Baby's tail.

It gave a few wags, but they were half-hearted at best. He'd interacted with Baby a lot while training Toaster. The dog was focused, but always wagging her tail.

"Which leg came up lame, Maria?" Violet looked at the woman.

She wiped a tear from her eye, then pointed

to her back left leg. "It doesn't bother her when I touch it. And she puts weight on it. But she pulls it up anytime she picks up speed."

Sliding around the table, Violet reached for the knee and moved it slowly. "It's an ACL tear." Violet set the leg back down. "I can feel the instability in the joint when I move it.

"She probably tore it coming off the A-frame. The initial pain was what caused her yelp. Luckily, it isn't overly painful now. It's sore, and if she moves wrong, she will feel the instability and some pain. I am going to prescribe pain meds. Then have our evening receptionist schedule a nonemergency surgery time for Ms. Baby." Violet snuggled her face close to the dog. "We'll get you feeling better in no time."

"Yes—" Maria shook her head "—but that means we are out for the season. You and Toaster are the alternates for the intermediate team. Looks like you're up, assuming you don't have any fancy trips planned."

"A weekend trip to Miami, but otherwise I am free until regionals. Toaster and I can step in." Nancy had wanted him on the intermediate team to begin with. But Beck hadn't wanted to commit. He'd taken the role as alternate and would keep the promise to the team. But he hated the reason he and Toaster were stepping in.

Maria took a deep breath. "I'll let the Nancy know."

"I'll handle it." Beck rubbed Baby's head." You focus on your girl. She is your priority."

"Tell that to Nancy." Maria rolled her eyes.

The agility gym owner, Nancy, was the definition of high stress. The woman was bent on winning. The only problem was the other members of the gym cared about their dogs' health and happiness, not ribbons and trophies.

The intermediate team competed in regionals, but they'd never placed. Something only Nancy ever complained about.

Maria rubbed Baby's head. "Let's get you home, sweet girl." She waited for Beck to lift Baby off the exam table, then led Baby out of the room.

"Toaster ready for a competition?" Violet asked as soon as the door closed.

"Yes. She loves the course. You should come." He held up his hand before she could offer the polite "no thanks" she'd given every other time he'd suggested she come to agility training.

The whole gym had been thrilled when Dr. Violet Lockwood moved to Maine. She'd started training agility dogs as a child, been a champion as a teen and one of the most sought-after coaches in South Florida.

Endorsements, coaching fees and a bestselling, at least in the agility circuit, book were how she'd paid her veterinarian school tuition. Then she'd just quit.

No reason given on the team social media channel she'd once made daily appearances on. Just a brief note to mention she'd parted ways with the South Beach Agility Training Group.

"We need to get to know each other a little better, if we are going to make your ex jealous." Beck was looking forward to learning more about the vet he spent so much time with but barely knew.

"I don't want to make him jealous. I just want to quiet any questions about my personal life." Violet crossed her arms, her chin rising just a little.

Damn she was fine.

"All right. That is your goal. *My* goal is to make him jealous." Beck pushed his hands into his scrub pockets.

"You have no reason to want to do that."

"He hurt you." Violet was one of the kindest people he'd ever met. And even if she wasn't, who texted…texted…their fiancée that it was over? An hour before they were supposed to get married.

That level of low deserved humbling. Period.

Rose crept up her cheeks as she broke eye contact. "Thank you."

His throat tightened as he stared at her. He coughed, trying to clear away the need rising around him. "Anyway, we need to look like a longtime couple to stave off the questions. I need to be at the event tomorrow evening, and we fly out in less than two weeks. The ruse needs to be perfect."

She bit her lip but then nodded. "I'll be there."

There was no way to stop the smile he felt creeping along his face. "It's a date."

"A fake date." Violet pointed a finger at him.

"A fake date," he conceded.

CHAPTER TWO

VIOLET RUBBED HER DOG, Bear's, head as she led him out of her car. The bully mix was around three. He'd been scrawny and missing most of his hair when she'd picked him at the shelter.

The all-white dog loved wearing sweaters, and Fiona had joked that Bear was Violet's dress-up doll the first time she sent his pictures to her. He was currently wearing a red shirt that said Stealing Hearts and Blasting Farts. It was the truest description of her big guy.

"You ready for tonight?" She looked at the training facility hosting this evening's team agility competition. It was tiny. Not even a third the size of the gym she and Thomas had owned in Miami. It had a homier look though.

Their third business partner, Mack, the one still on the title, had wanted everything sterile. Or as sterile as possible with dogs running around. Most agility dogs were family pets who loved to run courses. Their "trainers" were pet parents who wanted to engage extroverted dogs, find an outlet for animals that without a purpose would become destructive.

But at the highest level of the sport there were endorsements and cash prizes. It was a good living, if you could get there. And she had. With Thomas. They'd been sought after trainers; three of the dogs she'd trained had won national championships. Beating her ex's dog.

Thomas hadn't taken those wins well. And the gym hadn't won a national championship since she left.

Wins weren't what most people competed for. And it wasn't what most at the Happy Feet Dog Gym were after.

Beck had promised her that tonight they were only competing for a beat-up trophy that said Happy Retirement. It was an inside joke so old no one remembered how it had started. But the trophy was part of the gym's lore now, so it stayed.

"Vi!"

Her blood heated as she turned to wave to Beck and Toaster. The blue-eyed border collie was Beck's pride and joy. Bear started wagging his tail. Toaster was Bear's favorite at the dog park. Though he mistakenly believed he could keep up with the blue-eyed border collie as she raced around the dog park.

Bear always collapsed as soon as she put him in the back of the car. He wiggled his butt as Toaster stepped forward.

"Toaster is very excited to see you too, Bear." Beck rubbed Toaster's head and smiled at her.

He was in blue jeans that hugged his hips just right and blue T-shirt accenting the muscles on his arms. Her mouth watered as he rubbed Bear's head. If she hadn't sworn off relationships, she'd ask him out for real. A hot man who loved dogs was her kryptonite.

He probably kissed like a dream too. Slow, soft, then hard… Heat was pulsing in her cheeks. And other places.

Standing, he turned all his attention to her. "Can I kiss you?"

Her mouth fell open. Was her mind manifesting what she'd just imagined?

"Kiss your cheek, I mean." Beck cleared his throat and glanced away for a minute.

"My cheek?" Disappointment threatened to swallow her. This was no manifestation.

"We need to keep up appearances at the wedding. Pretending to be a happy couple now is probably good so awkward moments don't happen in Miami."

Awkward moments like this.

"Right." That made sense. Perfect sense. "Of course you can." She leaned forward a little, hoping the disappointment creeping along her spine would find its way out of her body.

The people in the gym knew them—or at least knew Beck. Knew he wasn't dating the ER veterinarian who went to work, home and the dog park. Violet was the definition of boring. She even had groceries delivered, now.

This hadn't been her plan. She and Thomas had traveled regularly on the training circuit. She'd even traveled overseas for several international competitions. Now though, her life was filled with work and nights in. She liked it—it would be nice if someone she cared about was beside her on the couch. But if Thomas had taught her anything, it was to not cede her peace to anyone.

Beck's lips were soft against her cheek. The touch gone too fast, but not quick enough for her body not to react.

She ran a hand down her neck, heat coating her fingertips as she tried to regain some composure. It was ridiculous to find such a quick moment so enticing. The man was playing her boyfriend, but that did not require her to act as though his touch lit a flame in her chest…and lower.

Beck wrapped an arm around her waist, but it felt more than a little off, as their dogs continued to jump and play together. "They look like they have been spending a lot of time together."

And we look awkward as hell.

She didn't voice that. She'd offered him the role of pretend boyfriend. Maybe Violet hadn't expected him to accept, but he had. Acting uncomfortable together wasn't going to achieve the goal she wanted.

In fact, it would stir up more questions. She'd started this adventure. She needed to see it through. Besides, a few weeks where she could touch Beck would hardly be a hardship.

"Can I kiss you?" She looked up at him.

He nodded, and she looked at him, drinking in the dimples on either side.

"Do I have something on my face?" Beck raised his left eyebrow.

"Just trying to decide which dimple to kiss." It was a silly statement but the truth.

"Personally, I suggest planting one on each, then deciding which is best." He leaned his left side forward, took her kiss, then turned the cheek and accepted one on his right. "So, which is the winning side?"

"Your left."

He made a tsking noise. "I always thought it was my right. Guess I've been posing in pictures on my bad side."

"You should rectify that." She hit his hip with hers, then pointed at the building. "Toaster needs to be warming up."

"Playing with Bear in the parking lot doesn't count?" There was that eyebrow raise again. Why did that motion make him look so dang cute?

"No. Do you usually have her jog around the perimeter, or up and down an A-frame a few times before starting her routine?" The words felt a little foreign. For years she'd spoken "agility" as a second language. A fluent recitation of workouts, routines, dog breeds and expectation management to unrealistic clients.

His deep chuckle stopped her in her tracks. "I don't have a standard routine. I am not sure any of us besides Nancy do. We compete in regionals because it is a fun trip out of state. And these Tuesday night competitions are less about competition and more about the potluck after."

"Potluck?" No one had told her about a potluck.

"No worries, I made a vat of chili." Beck squeezed her side.

"A vat?"

"Yes. It means large pot." He chuckled as she knocked her hip, a little harder than last time, against his. "The point is, I made a huge thing of chili that I dropped off a little while ago and picked up a thing of your favorite cookies at the store and brought them under your name. I wasn't risking letting you back out of coming tonight."

"How do you know my favorite cookie?" Violet let him open the door. She made Bear sit, waiting until the bully mix settled enough to follow the command, gave him a praise, then a hand command to walk through the door.

Beck did the same with Toaster, who obediently followed the command immediately.

"See how easy she makes it look?" Violet pointed to Toaster, who now seemed 100-percent focused on the training environment. Border col-

lies were lovely pups, but the breed was bred to
work. She always advised first-time dog owners
to choose a less energetic breed to learn the ropes
of dog ownership.

"Bear follows commands. He just takes a minute to think it over." Beck ran his hand along
Bear's head, scratching behind her ears.

"Uh-huh." Violet gave Bear a playful scold-
ing look, then turned her attention back to Beck.
It was true though. Bear was very well-behaved.
"You didn't answer. How do you know my favorite cookie?"

"You hide a box of chocolate-dipped short-
bread cookies above your desk in the same cabinet where the extra-small and extra-large gloves
are stored. Not the best hiding place. We all know
they are there."

"I'm not hiding them from you guys. I'm hiding them from me." She let out a huff. She'd actually forgotten that was where she'd stored them
a month and half ago. She'd torn out the bottom
drawer of her desk certain she'd eaten them in the
fog after a difficult ER patient.

She'd dated Thomas for two years, been engaged for two more and the man had insisted that
her favorite cake was red velvet whenever anyone
asked. Red velvet was a fine cake but the answer
today was the same as it had been then—devil's
food cake. She doubted her ex-fiancé paid any attention to the fancy cookies she purchased once a

month, then hoarded for tough days to add a ray of sunlight.

And yet, Beck had noticed. Noticed and made sure there was a pack here tonight with her name on them.

"Thank you."

"No problem." He raised a hand, then pointed to the A-frame. "Vi says you need to warm up, and she is the expert. So let's go, girl." He offered Violet a small wave, then took Toaster out onto the field.

The man was sweet. And no one was ever going to say that watching him walk away in jeans hugging his perfect ass was a hardship.

Beck ran Toaster through her paces. Careful not to look over at Violet too often. The woman was like a magnet. The entire gym seemed to have found its way into her perimeter.

The expert they'd sought for years was finally here. From this vantage point it seemed like she was enjoying herself. He didn't want to hover. Vi could take care of herself, but as Nancy Perkins strode toward the vet, he motioned for Toaster to follow him.

Nancy was the gym's agility club president. The only one whose dog competed in competitions outside of regionals, and occasionally medaled. Never won, though. A complaint that was never far from Nancy's lips.

She'd not been quiet about her frustrations at Vi's continued refusal to join the gym. Even when everyone pointed out that Violet's schedule at the ER clinic made it difficult to be here when the gym was open and that her responses were always courteous. She'd written the book on the sport, literally, with what he now suspected was the ex-fiancé.

Stepping away from something was okay. As was rejoining…if you felt like it.

"Dr. Lockwood, good of you to *finally* join us."

Beck got to Violet's side just as Nancy let out the passive aggressive greeting.

"What finally brings you into our humble midst?" If Nancy was trying to win over the agility coach that had led multiple teams to international championships, this was the least likely way to accomplish it.

"I heard there was a big vat of delicious chili here." Violet met his gaze, her bright jeweled eyes glittering with her *What the f...* look he sometimes saw when pet parents made choice for their living breathing family member that made no sense.

"I don't know about delicious." He winked and slipped onto the bench next to her, wrapping an arm around her waist. They were playing pretend boyfriend and girlfriend, so the motion made sense. But he'd pulled her close because he didn't like the tone Nancy was taking.

Nancy's gaze slipped to his hand before she smiled. "So you're helping Toaster tonight?"

"I'm just here for the chili. And to root for my…" Her voice faltered as she looked away. "Root Beck on." Vi cleared her throat, then ran a hand over his knee.

His body flooded with need at the simple touch. "Why don't you come with me onto the course with Toaster? She needs to warm up more."

He stood, and Violet followed.

"Think Bear wants to come too?"

"You know he is too lazy for it." Vi wrapped her arm around his waist, squeezing him before letting go. The ghost of her touch clung to him.

Getting touched by Violet Lockwood over the next few weeks was not going to be a hardship.

"He likes the A-frame at the dog park." He couldn't help the chuckle that followed the phrase.

Vi playfully rolled her eyes to the ceiling. What Bear liked was barking at the dogs that ran up the A-frame, then running around it before lying under the shade. Bear had energy…when Bear wanted.

Otherwise he was perfectly content to lie around all day. Toaster was the exact opposite!

"All right, why don't you send her through the whole course." Vi gestured to the course, then made a hand sign to Bear. The sweet pittie sat, then lay down, putting his head on his front paws and letting out a friendly bark at Toaster.

"Looks like you have a cheering section." Beck snapped his fingers three times and headed toward the starting area. He usually ran Toaster through the course one full time before she actually ran the course, just for familiarization.

She took off through the weave polls, then headed onto the seesaw, before hitting top speed at the first tunnel. She jumped over the single jump, the double, then flew through the hanging tire. When she pulled up at the end, Violet clapped.

Violet walked over, and he saw several people looking their way. Probably wondering how he'd found a way to get the famously hermit-like veterinarian to train Toaster. No one had asked about them arriving together, but the gym's gossips would be talking soon.

Hopefully their short fake dalliance wouldn't cause any issues. That was a potential problem for future Beck—his favorite activity was putting off tough issues to his future self. His mother had always said not to put off hard things... Beck saw no reason to accept difficulties until you absolutely had too. After all, the worries might disappear all on their own.

He caught Nancy leaning on the wall, carefully trying to catch any advice Vi might give him. She was going to be disappointed. Toaster didn't need training. His girl was having a blast, and so was he.

Beck was never motivated by prizes. It was the experience he craved. His mother had gotten unexpectedly pregnant with him in her late forties. His father was in his late fifties. They'd been thrilled after trying to get pregnant for years and losing the few pregnancies they'd had.

His parents had loved him deeply, but anything that might be slightly dangerous was not something they signed him up for.

Soccer…knee and concussion issues.

Football…traumatic brain injuries.

Swim team…drowning from exhaustion.

Gymnastics…broken necks.

They'd cared for him so much, but it wasn't until after he moved out that he got to try new things. Beck was motivated by the adrenaline rush.

"She looks like she is having fun." Vi stepped next to him. "And you positively beam when you are running with her."

"It's fun. Didn't you enjoy it when you ran the gym in Miami?" It was the wrong question. The second it was out of his mouth, she frowned, looking over her shoulder.

"I thought I did." Violet let out a small sigh.

"Vi?"

"What time does the competition start? I am looking forward to your chili." The words were clipped. She was not going to discuss Miami. Even though they were headed there soon.

Into the heart of a past she clearly didn't want to step into.

Reaching for her hand, he pulled her palm into his. She squeezed it but didn't drop the connection. So he took it a step closer and pulled her to him, wrapping his arms around her.

She leaned her head against his shoulder as he hugged her. He held her, looking at the clock. He'd read that twenty-second hugs were ideal to lower cortisol—the stress hormone.

After about fifteen seconds she let out a long sigh, but he didn't let go. Finally, she took a deep breath and stepped out of his embrace. "You didn't answer my question. What time does it start?"

"All right, everyone, let's get this started." Nancy clapped her hands and pointed to Bear. "If this one is participating, you need to join the gym. We can do paperwork after the competition."

"Just the cheering section." Violet snapped her fingers, and Bear stood. "Good luck." She brushed her lips against his, the touch barely there, but for a split second everything and everyone around him disappeared.

Violet snapped her fingers again, and she and Bear started walking to the stands.

Callie, one of his friends, stepped up beside him. "You two are positively glowing. I even snapped a pic of it. So cute. I'll send it to you."

She clapped her hands. "Guess now I know why you've turned down all my attempts to set you up."

Before he could find the words to explain why this was just fun, Callie was already dancing away. The woman was collectively known as the gym's worst matchmaker. Not a single pairing she'd orchestrated had ever worked out. But that didn't mean Callie was giving up.

She'd tried for the last year to find him a date. She was convinced he'd be happiest if he settled down. Maybe...one day.

He looked over at Violet. She raised a hand, giving a thumbs-up. He could feel the heat in his cheeks. The ghost of her lips against his.

Vi was kind. Great with animals. One of the smartest people he'd ever met. She was gorgeous, inside and out. But he wasn't looking for a partner.

Not now. Maybe not ever.

His parents had traveled the world. In fact, they'd met each other while hiking the Tour De Mont Blanc. They'd met in France and been head over heels in love by the time they'd crossed the Italian border.

His father had told him the story a million times. Stars in his eyes as he looked over at this mother. To hear his dad say it, they'd "gotten boring" after that. Bought a cottage in Bangor, Maine.

His father had taken a job at the University of

Maine as a professor of anthropology. His mother had worked as a civil engineer for the city of Bangor, creating a more sustainable city with winters that spent weeks well below freezing.

After they married the adventures were just retold stories in faded photographs and memories. That was not how he was going to live his life.

CHAPTER THREE

THE BACK DOOR CHIMED, and Violet didn't need to look over her shoulder to know that Beck had just walked into the clinic. The day techs finished an hour after Dr. Brown, and the other day shift veterinarians, so they could catch her up on any patients that would be staying with her until her shift ended at two.

Her cheeks heated as she listened to his footsteps come closer. She'd kissed him last night. Sort of. Her lips had brushed his just before he headed to the "competition."

Even now her fingers itched to trace her lips at the memory…something she'd done more than she wanted to remember last night.

"Hope you're hungry." Beck stepped to her side and dropped three glass bowls filled with chili. "I have lots of leftovers and no room left in my freezer, so I packed up dinner."

The top bowl had Lacey's name on it. That wasn't surprising; Beck seemed incapable of not considering others. Their receptionist worked the same late hours they did.

He bent his head, and for a moment she thought he was going to kiss her. She lifted her head, the motion automatic, and pursed her lips as he instead grabbed the bowl with Lacey's name and headed out.

Fire roasted her cheeks. Seriously. What was wrong with her? Yes, she'd kept herself walled off from relationships. Walled off was an understatement. She'd accepted exactly two dates in the last year. Both epic failures.

But it wasn't like she was looking for anything special.

One failed engagement that resulted in so much fallout was more than enough to make sure you paid close attention to the person you were with. Sure she was lonely sometimes, or all the time. But loneliness was the price of keeping heartbreak at bay.

She'd missed every red flag with Thomas. And there had been *a lot*. That was a mistake she had no intention of making again.

Beck ignited a fire in her body despite all her intentions to keep her heart flame free. Probably because he was so hot. Physical attraction and years of self-induced celibacy were finally catching up to her.

"You feeling better about the wedding now?" Beck opened the door to the back room, placed his hand on the top of the door frame and leaned forward.

Damn. It took every ounce of willpower not to lick her lips at the sight.

Swallowing the lump of desire crawling up her throat, Violet looked at the notes from the day in front of her. "I've checked with the sitter for Bear. I know Julie is watching Toaster too. I hope she is ready to have our two plus her Pepper in the mix. They might have a wild weekend. My neighbor is going to water my plants. All I really have left is packing."

"That isn't what I meant."

She knew that. Knew he hadn't been checking to see if her bridesmaid dress was hung in the travel bag to avoid wrinkles or if the makeup she was using for the wedding was picked out and her town house ready to be empty for a few days.

"I don't know." Honesty. That was one way to handle this, maybe even the best way. But she hated the shame hovering in the three words. It had been years. It shouldn't matter that Thomas was going to be there. Shouldn't matter that he'd found someone who looked just like her. Some-one he'd showed up to marry.

"It's okay to be nervous." Beck didn't come closer, no hug today like there'd been yesterday. That was fine.

"I'm not nervous." She bit her lip. "I'm pissed."

Violet blew out a breath. There was that honesty again.

"I mean…" Words failed to materialize.

"You mean?" Now Beck was moving toward her. His dark blue eyes trained on her.

Balling her hands, she tried to find words. What the hell, she'd uttered the truth out loud, may as well finish the conversation. "I lost so much when Thomas ended our relationship. He took all our stuff; pushed me out of our agility business. He even got Gran's holiday tablecloth. I mean why would even want my Gran's holiday cloth? That was just spite."

Violet felt like she was vibrating as words she hadn't let spill forth for years bubbled over. "He kept his head high while I cried over what I thought was a loving relationship only to realize I'd played the fool."

Besides losing the one family heirloom she cared about, that was the toughest part. Once he was gone, it was easy to see where all the cracks were. Easy to see why Fiona had checked not once, but three times in the month leading up to her wedding if she was really sure she wanted to do this.

At the time, Violet thought her friend was just worried she'd get cold feet. But nope.

She hadn't come from a loving home. Her parents stayed together for years out of spite. No one had wanted to lose face in the community for "breaking" their family. The lawyers had been hired right after Violet had graduated high school.

Even growing up watching an unhappy couple muddle through, she'd been so certain that she'd found true love.

Then he just walked away. If she'd had an inkling, any suspicion, maybe it wouldn't have been as hard.

But the truth was he'd always hated that she was too successful in their shared field to truly keep her under his thumb in the way that he'd wanted. No matter how small she learned to make herself it was never enough for his ego. But she understood it now. Had learned to look and evaluate every step. She was not losing herself again. Never again.

"I don't miss him, but man I wish I was the one going to this wedding with a new spouse on my arm, rather than dragging a fake date with me. No offense."

"None taken." Beck's arm wrapped around her shoulders, giving her a quick, tight, work-appropriate squeeze. "First of all, you're not dragging me. In fact, if I remember correctly, you tried very hard to take back an invitation that I jumped at."

She rolled her eyes.

"Careful. My mom always told me if I rolled my eyes too hard, they'd get stuck like that."

Beck only chuckled as she stuck her tongue out him.

"Second, no way for us to walk in married. The courthouse is already closed." He chuckled but never stopped watching her.

Her mouth was hanging open, even though she knew he'd offered the statement as a joke.

"But we can be dating. That way it isn't fake."

Violet's ears were ringing, and she wasn't sure he was making any sense. "Wha—"

"Vi, will you go on a date with me? A real one, besides to an agility gym?"

They'd acted the couple at the agility course last night. The simple kisses in the parking lot should have been the end of it. But she'd found herself reaching for his hand or enjoying it as his arm wrapped around her waist. Beck beside her while Nancy was a giant pill was nice, even when she'd failed to describe what they were to each other.

Last night was unexpected but comfortable. She did not want to tarnish that memory.

"I don't want a pity date, Beck. But I appreciate the offer."

His hands cupped her cheeks. "This is not a pity date. You are fantastic, Vi. Brilliant, funny, kind, pretty. I would *love* to take you out."

He'd called her pretty last. It was a silly thing to focus on, but everyone called her gorgeous. She knew she was conventionally attractive. Long wavy dark hair, a slim figure, high cheekbones. All things society deemed "special."

But those were also genetic things that she had no control over.

"You are very sweet."

Beck held up a hand. "I know a brush-off when I hear one, and I won't push, but we can go as people who are dating. It doesn't have to be exclusive. We can have a no strings attached fling that is just for fun. Your friends don't have to know it just started."

A fling. With Beck. Her toes curled in her sneakers as she tried to ignore the heat flashing through her body.

"Sounds pretty good to me." She popped a hand over her mouth as the words hung between them. Oh my. She'd meant to keep those words inside her head.

Both his dimples appeared as he raised his eyebrows again. "It *does* sound like a good idea."

Violet looked at Beck; he seemed genuinely interested. Dating a man ten years her junior was not something Vi ever planned to do. But returning to a wedding where her ex was wasn't on her bucket list either. They *were* going away for the weekend.

Once upon a time, Violet would have jumped at the chance to just have fun. To experience the moment.

Damn she missed that woman sometimes.

But that woman got hurt. That woman got her heart trampled. Still…

"Yes. I would very much enjoy going on a date with you. But—"

"Vi—"

"Hold on." She held up a hand. "We are co-workers. We should probably have some ground rules."

"Not a terrible idea." Beck reached for the hand she'd held up. He squeezed it quickly, then released it. "Rule one…"

Before he could finish that sentence, three quick buzzes rang over the speaker. That was the code for emergency.

She took off, knowing Beck was on her heels.

"My cat was hit by a car." A young man, no more than nineteen, was holding a small box.

"We'll do the best we can." Beck offered kind words, but she knew by the shift in his shoulders that the outcome was all but certain. He took the cat to the back to start vitals and triage.

"Lacey—"

"I'll get a room ready." A goodbye room. She didn't say those words, but the young man seemed to understand what was going on.

"Let's go over some options, while my vet tech looks at—"

"Minnow. His name is Minnow. Found him while I was fishing when I was fourteen. He was scrawny and in bad need of a bath, I didn't think my momma would let me keep him but…"

"Minnow is very lucky to have you." Violet

took a deep breath. Tonight was going to be a rough shift—the life of an emergency vet.

Beck pulled up to Don's. The hideaway bar was relaxing, and on Sunday evenings Don hooked up a karaoke machine. It drew in an eclectic crowd.

It wasn't his typical first date hangout. But this wasn't a typical first date—and he was stunned Vi was even still willing to come out after yesterday's shift.

They'd lost the cat hit by the car, and two other emergencies had come in that were still very touch and go. It was one of those shifts that could make you question your choice in careers.

So he'd chosen Don's. Because it was tiny and people left you alone. And most importantly it was easy to lose any unhappy thoughts in the chaos that was people screeching out tunes. And given that Halloween wasn't all that far off, there was bound to be at least one silly rendition of "Monster Mash" every night.

"Beck." Vi held up a hand as she walked over from her bright yellow SUV. The car would never get lost in a crowded parking lot. Not that Bangor had too many of those.

She was dressed in jeans and a bright red sweater. "Let's get inside." Vi grinned as she hustled toward the door.

He followed. "You know most people wear coats once September is in the rearview mirror."

October days were still decently mild, but the evenings were chilly and it was windy tonight.

Vi rubbed her hands up her arms as they moved toward the bar. "I hate bringing a coat into a restaurant or bar."

Beck put his arm around her shoulders to add some extra warmth to her. "There's the coat rack." He pointed to the corner where the hangers were already filling with brightly, and not so brightly, colored coats.

"My dad used to forget our coats when we were going out. Mostly to piss off my mom. She was very controlling and…" Vi shrugged. "I got used to just running into places when it was cold. They were always going to fight, but at least it wasn't going to be about my coat."

Vi chuckled as she leaned against the bar and ordered a beer. Beck didn't know what to say. That was clearly a story she'd told before, one she might even think was funny. But it was disturbing.

"You grew up in Maine?" He'd been born in Bangor. Graduated from Bangor High School, gone to vet tech school at the University of Maine Augusta campus…in Bangor and now lived in the home he'd been raised in. He traveled frequently. His passport was filling with stamps, and he'd visited thirty of the fifty US states already. But somehow, the home coated with happy memories with his parents was where he always came back to.

"No." Violet thanked the bartender as she held up her beer and headed for a booth on the back wall.

He grabbed his drink and followed.

Sliding into the booth, Vi took a deep sip of her drink, then let out a sigh. "I grew up in Kansas. So not as much snow as here, but the wind in the winter BITES. Nothing but flat land so no wind breaks. I moved to Florida for college, and to put more than a thousand miles between my parents and me."

Once more she'd stunned the words from him. His parents had protected him—a little too much. But he'd never wanted distance between them. Even now, he had several pictures of their adventures in his living room so he could feel close to them on the days when his soul ached that all he had left was their memory.

"All of that is information I don't normally share on a first date." She looked at her beer, spinning the bottle around by its neck. "But it's information Fiona would expect you to have."

"Right." Somehow the fact that he needed to pass the boyfriend test at least one of her friends would throw his way had slipped his mind.

"Do you have a coat in the car, at least?" This part of Maine was no stranger to poor weather even in October. People started making sure their trunks had coats, blankets and kitty litter you could put under your tires to create friction against ice if you slid off the road at the end of September.

"Of course." Vi's nose twitched and she pursed her lips. "It's nearly winter."

"Give me your keys." He held out his hand.

Vi kept spinning the beer bottle. "Why?"

"Because I am going to grab your coat. We'll hang it right by mine. So it's nice and warm when you go outside."

"Beck, it's fine."

"No." He shook his hand. "Your keys, Vi."

She rolled her eyes but fished them out of her jeans pocket. "It's not necessary."

Beck tilted his head. "I think we have very different ideas of necessary in this situation. I promise I won't let you forget it."

Running outside, he grinned as he pulled open her SUV's door. She had two key chains hanging from a lanyard on her rear view mirror. One said, *Therapy isn't enough. I need to bite people.* The other was a coffee cup that read, *My blood type is coffee.*

The lanyard with the key chains fit the bright yellow car. He grabbed the coat off the passenger seat and headed back in. After hanging it on the hook next to his, he headed back to his date.

"If I forget my coat, I am never letting *you* forget it." She playfully wagged a finger at him, then looked up at the stage as the first karaoke performer started up.

He wasn't going to let her forget her coat. But there was a more important issue at hand now.

"We have to have a bet."

"A bet?"

There wasn't time for a long explanation. "When will someone sing 'Monster Mash'? Three songs in? Five in? Last of the night? It's October, the holiday tune *will* come up."

Vi covered her mouth, but her eyes were bright with a smile. "'Monster Mash'?" She looked at the performer, flipping through the song book.

"I say it's between the fourth and eighth performance." Beck leaned a little closer, enjoying the happiness radiating from her.

"I say the last one, or the last one we are here for. I know we usually work the night shift, but closing the bar down on our night off is no guarantee."

"Fair." He'd spend as much time as she wanted at the bar. But he also understood the need to head home after decompressing.

The first song started, "Bohemian Rhapsody."

"That is ambitious!" Vi looked at the singer, then turned back to him. "What are we betting for? Usually that is decided before the bet is even outlined, but we had to rush tonight."

"Who kisses who first." Beck winked.

Kiss. Her mouth went dry. He wasn't talking

about the soft, barely there kiss she'd given him the other night. No, this was a real kiss.

"What is rule one, Beck?" She needed to think of something other than how his mouth would feel against hers.

He raised an eyebrow.

"You said it before Minnow..." Violet bit her lip, then took a swig of her drink. Veterinarian work was incredibly rewarding. Unfortunately, it could also be devastating—particularly for those who worked in emergency med. The hard cases stayed with you.

"Right." Beck shook his head. "Rule one is I never plan to marry. Or at least not until I am old...like thirty-five." It was his standard statement and joke. The thirty-five was a number he and a friend had chosen in college. Nothing serious, but he saw the hurt flash across Vi's eyes.

"Damn it. Sorry, Vi. It's a joke. I always add the age, and I wasn't thinking and I..." Wow he was digging a hole but couldn't seem to get his brain to stop spitting words. "I don't think you are old."

"It's fine, Beck." Vi shrugged. "I thought thirty-five was old too when I was twenty-six. It seemed very far off. Then I blinked and." She gestured to herself.

The woman was fine. And not fine like everything is fine. But F-I-N-E. She was gorgeous and he'd just jammed his foot in his mouth.

"The good news is that I don't have any immediate plans to race to the aisle." She let out a sigh. "One failed trip to that altar is enough to make one supercautious. This is a fling, remember." She pulled his free hand into hers. Her fingers twisting through his.

Heat shot through him as her thumb traced circles on this wrist.

"So key chains?" He pulled her hand to his lips.

"Oh." Violet let out a giggle. "I have no idea how that happened but I love them. I used to pick one up every place I traveled. Now any that make me laugh come home with me. My collection is well over a hundred at this point."

"Nice. I don't really have a collection of anything. Well, coffee mugs. But those are holdovers from Mom, mostly." His father had bought any mug his mother wanted, and she'd wanted a lot of them. Silly phrases—yep. Innuendos—of course. Looked like it belonged in the trash already—she'd love it.

"I need another drink. A water this time. You want anything?" She squeezed his hand, then pulled back.

"I'll get it." Beck needed a moment to gather his thoughts. Find a way to make sure he didn't utter any more stupid jokes tonight.

Violet clapped as the singer finished the angry breakup song. The singer's girlfriends were all cheering in the booth next to them.

"No need to be a body language expert to know she is going through it." Beck squeezed her arm.

He'd slid into the side of the booth with her about an hour an ago. They'd chatted about their backstories and silly things. It was relaxing, despite his initial faux pas about age.

She let out a yawn and he smiled. "I think that might be our signal to call it a night."

"We can't. You lost the bet but if we leave now, it's a draw." She yawned again.

"We'll just have to table the bet for another night. You are exhausted, Vi."

Competition flared through her. She hadn't felt the bite of it for years. Since Thomas and she went their own ways. But the glow was there now.

"Come on." She grabbed his hand and pulled them out of the booth. She was winning the bet.

Heading toward the stage she quickly flipped through the book, found the number for "Monster Mash," and pushed the code into the machine. There were two mics, so she handed one to him and grabbed the other.

Beck was laughing. "Vi, I can't sing. I'm terrible at it."

"Well, then it is a good thing for you that this is karaoke night. No one is expecting perfection!"

The musical bars started playing, and she waited for the words to start appearing on screen. "I thought you always jumped at experiences."

Beck playfully threw a hand over his chest. "You wound me, dear lady."

Her laughter nearly made her miss the song's first words.

The three minute song was over too fast. As the music cut out the giggles started. "I guess I win."

"I guess you do." Beck took her mic, his fingers grazing her wrist.

She'd had exactly two beers in the three hours they'd been there. She was sober, but as his blue gaze met hers, she nearly swooned.

Two women stepped up to the book of available songs, and she grabbed his hand. "Come on, we have to go before their song starts or we both lose."

"I didn't realize you were so competitive." Beck wrapped an arm around her waist as they headed to the coat rack.

"I used to be really competitive. It was why I was such a good agility trainer. It made me feel alive." She slipped into her coat and waited for Beck to grab his.

The bars of the next song were starting as they hit the door, but the words hadn't started, so she was going to keep the win.

She walked to her car. The night was cool, but compared to what was coming in the next few weeks, it was balmy. Something her Florida friends would not have agreed with.

"So since I won the bet, do I get to kiss you or

you kiss me? We never actually spelled out the terms, which looking back at it was an oversight." She was giddy. Violet couldn't remember the last time she felt like this.

No, she could. Her bachelorette party. They'd danced on tables, at a location where that was allowed. It was an experience and she'd jumped at it. Easily.

She hadn't been that person in so long.

"I think as the winner you get to decide. Do you want to kiss me?" He leaned against the door of her SUV, his gaze never leaving hers. "Or do you want me to kiss you?"

Her brain short-circuited. Both options were amazing. Both options heated her skin. There was literally no wrong answer.

Violet looked toward the entrance of the bar as a couple walked out laughing. She missed that kind of companionship. The excitement of someone next to you.

This was a fling. Something fun. But even the idea of it was awakening something she'd kept dormant since forever.

"I want you to kiss me." Violet held up her head, expecting Beck's lips to capture hers immediately.

Instead, he leaned his arm against her SUV. Then he put his other arm around her waist. His sweet, honeyed gaze swept over her. Sounds echoed around them as others headed to their cars, but they were far away. Like somehow, Beck had slipped them into a world all their own.

His fingers spread on her back as he looked at her. "You are so perfect." The arm on the SUV drew the loose hair away from her eyes.

"Beck." She breathed out his name. Violet had never had someone stare at her as though nothing else in the world mattered. As though they could look at her forever and never tire of the image.

Her knees felt like they might buckle and heat filled her cheeks. "Kiss me."

This time, he didn't hesitate. His lips brushed hers, then the hand on her back pulled her closer and he deepened the kiss.

There was nothing rooting her to the ground. Everything in this moment was Beck. Her mouth opened and his tongue grazed hers. His hands ran up and down her back, drawing her even closer.

Her body crashed to the ground as he pulled back.

"I had fun tonight, Vi." He wasn't kissing her, but his arms still held her tightly.

"Me, too. We'll have to come back here some-time." The words spilled out and she bit her lip. This was a fling. Kisses and a date to a wedding. It wasn't a plan anything kind of relationship.

"I'd like that." Beck kissed the top of her head, then stepped back. "Have a lovely evening, Vi."

CHAPTER FOUR

BECK STRETCHED BEFORE he walked into the clinic. He was going to see Vi. At work.

That last part was important. This was work. The place they were keeping separate. It was something they'd agreed on the other night at Don's. At work they were colleagues.

When the fling was over, they still had to work together. He'd readily agreed, but that was before he'd kissed her. The taste of her had lingered for hours. Or maybe his brain had just latched on to the perfection that was Vi and refused to let the happiness go.

As he walked into the clinic he waved to Lacey, then headed toward the back room. The receptionist was wearing cat ears. Halloween was still more than three weeks away, but Lacey loved the holiday and started dressing up as different animals on October 1. The cat ears were actually pretty tame compared to her usual monthly attire.

"Hi, Beck." Violet was looking in on Patches, a small dog that had come in the same night as

Minnow. Patches was dehydrated for reasons they hadn't been able to figure out.

Looking over Vi's shoulder, he couldn't stop the smile. Patches was wagging her tail and standing right by the door of her enclosure.

"Someone looks better."

"Right." Vi turned. Her dark hair was up in a messy bun today, and she was grinning from ear to ear. "Her panels came back clean, so I think it was a viral infection."

"You gave your parents a very big scare, little one." Beck wagged a finger at the enclosure. Patches offered a yip and more tail wags.

"Right." Vi shook her head. "I told her the same thing. The good news is they are on their way to get her. Happy times."

"Those are the best times." Beck leaned against the counter. "Did you see Lacey's cat ears? Is it wrong that the easiness of today's costumes makes me wonder what we will see her in on Halloween?"

Vi shook her head. "No. I asked her what her costume is for Halloween and she said it was a secret. I reminded her that Halloween tends to be very busy and she needs to be able to move easily."

"So no giraffe repeat?" Last year Lacey had barely been able to get into the office with the papier-mâché head she'd built for the costume.

"Right." Violet moved over to the other pup

they'd been monitoring for several days. Patches looked significantly better; Nix did not.

The gray cat was curled up in a ball in the back of the enclosure. He barely lifted his head when Violet reached in.

"His panels are also back. Kidney disease."

Given the cat's advanced age, that didn't surprise Beck. It still sucked.

"I already let Linda know. She bought some beds so he is more comfy since jumping up into her bed is harder now. She is going to switch his food and just love on him for as long as possible." Vi rubbed Nix's head. The cat let out a low purr but didn't raise his head.

The pager on his hip buzzed. "Looks like the first patient of the night is here." Beck sent a silent hope up that such an early arrival didn't mean they were in for a long night.

He stepped into the room to see a young woman holding a small dog. The little guy was shaking, and Beck blinked twice. The black dog had a stripe on his nose and a white patch on his chest. The dog looked just like his childhood pet, Lolly.

He took a deep breath and offered a smile to the worried pet parent. "I'm Beck, the vet tech. What brings you in tonight?"

"My mom brought over my gran's rocking chair." She let out a soft sob. "Gran passed last month and I love the rocker."

"Of course." Beck nodded. The dog looked like

it was in pain, but it wasn't bleeding. If the woman didn't get to the point shortly, he'd redirect her.

"I was rocking in it. Remembering Gran. I had my eyes closed and—" she let out a sob "—the next thing I heard was Bug screech."

She bit her lip so hard, Beck feared she was tasting blood.

"Okay. Do you know what part of Bug was under the rocking chair?"

"His tail."

Beck took a step closer and Bug snarled at him. Not an unexpected reaction. Small dogs were notoriously feisty despite their size, and an injured animal was always more prone to strike first and ask questions later.

"I am going to muzzle Bug so I can get a good look at him." Beck pulled the muzzle out of the cabinet.

The owner held up her hand and he prepped himself to explain why muzzles were good for Bug and the staff. "I can do it. I've muzzled him at our regular vet before. He isn't a full Chihuahua, but he has many of their traits."

She took the muzzle from his hand, got it on Bug, then gently passed her little boy over to him. It was easy to see the damage to the tail.

"Oh. You poor guy." Beck spoke softly to Bug, even as the tiny dog voiced his obvious displeasure at being held, the muzzle and his tail. "I am going to take Bug to get X-rays. Dr. Lockwood will want to see what is happening there."

The woman let out a soft sob and curled into herself.

As he started toward the door, Beck turned. "This isn't your fault. Promise."

"Lacey says Nola is having a cup of tea, but she doesn't want to leave until after the surgery is completed." Violet looked at Bug's X-rays one more time. The rocking chair had crushed his tail almost at the base.

Tail crushes weren't always an emergency. Sometimes they could give the pup pain meds and do surgery during regular business hours. But X-rays indicated Bug's tail crush was causing nerve damage. The longer the pressure was on the nerve, the more likely Bug was going to suffer long-term consequences.

She turned and looked at Beck. He was bent over Bug, carefully monitoring the dog's breathing. "How is Bug?"

Beck looked up and nodded. "Good. He is fully under, and his heart rate is staying steady."

"Excellent." Violet went to the sink, washed up and donned gloves. "I hate having to amputate his tail, but that nerve damage might hurt his back."

"He will be the cutest boy with the bobtail. Then he really will look just like my Lolly." Beck rubbed a gloved finger over Bug's ear.

"Lolly?" Violet stepped to the table and picked up the scalpel. She took one quick breath before starting the surgery.

"Lolly was my puppy growing up. I found her at the university behind a garbage can when I was waiting for my dad to get out of a meeting. I was seven. Lolly was probably two or three. She had a bobtail and looked just like this guy." Beck tilted his head, and she knew he was seeing a dog he loved and had to say goodbye to.

"You had a small dog and now you have an agility border collie? Did you want a big dog and your parents wouldn't let you have one?" Her mother had been against having a dog.

"No. Lolly found me, and Toaster was too much for her first owner. Border collies don't do well in shelters. Destruction is their go-to the moment they are bored." It was nice that Beck was willing to have dogs of all sizes. She was partial to large dogs, but that didn't mean if the right small pup showed up, she wouldn't jump at that opportunity too.

Nope. That mental thought felt a little too close to seeing a future. They were having a fun fling. Rushing into thoughts like that was how she'd gotten stood up at the aisle years ago. She shouldn't need the reminder.

"Did you parents do agility?"

It shouldn't be an awkward question, but then so much about growing up she found awkward as

an adult. The stories she'd told as family lore—
fights over coats, or learning to climb onto the top
of the fridge when her parents were arguing so if
any glass got broken she didn't step on it, or that
time her mom asked her dad to pick her up and
she got left at school because he swore she hadn't
asked and neither wanted to admit the other was
right—weren't as silly as she'd thought they were.

"No. My mom didn't want a dog. I wanted one
so bad. I asked for a puppy every year at Christmas from the time I was thirteen when Yoshi
showed up under the tree. Mom was not pleased.
She said the first time he did something bad it
was right off to the shelter with him."

The memory of her starting to cry and her father starting to yell at her mother echoed through
her soul. Her father had gotten the dog for all the
wrong reasons. Her mother was heartless about
anyone else's feelings. And she'd been a kid who'd
just gotten warned she could lose her puppy anytime. Even with all that, it had still been her happiest Christmas.

"I trained him so there was no reason Mom
could give to get rid of him. Then I found that I
liked it."

Violet smiled behind her mask. "Yoshi and I
won regionals, then youth nationals. I lost him
when I was a senior in college. By then he'd
stopped doing agility work and I was compet-

ing with Pebbles, but in a world of good boys, he was the bestest."

"You got into agility to keep your mom from giving away your dog?" It didn't matter that he was wearing a mask, she could see the frown through his eyes.

"My mom needed control. She got meds for anxiety after a breakdown about four years ago. It's better. Now, she lives in Arizona, owns her own pottery shop and is dating someone who I think makes her genuinely happy."

Now that her mother's mental health had been addressed, it hurt that the woman she was now would have been a good mother. That woman would have loved her dearly. Violet had forgiven her, but they would never be close.

"My father isn't exactly a saint in this story. He knew my mother didn't want an animal in the house. In her defense, he never helped with a lick of housework. The man was weaponized incompetence personified." Getting a puppy out of spite was pretty much the worst reason to get another living creature. The fact that it had worked out was due more to Violet's stubbornness than anything else.

"Wow."

She couldn't fault Beck for not having anything else to add to that conversation. "How often did your parents fight?"

Violet looked at the bone around the tail. Hoping to find a way to save more of it.

"Very rarely. I remember they argued once when Dad wanted me to join soccer. Or rather Dad was tired of me pestering him about me joining soccer. Mom didn't agree."

"The team too expensive?" Violet had played lacrosse and her parents had supported her, though they stood on opposite sides of the field when they attended games together.

"Too dangerous." Beck let out a chuckle that had little humor behind it. "All sports were too dangerous. I guess after finally having me, they weren't willing to risk losing me. But I never had to hop up on the counter to avoid flying glass."

"Oh." Violet frowned as the tail's full damage came into view.

"What's going on?" Beck looked at the array of displays showing Bug's status. "He is still holding on well. Heart rate steady. Breathing normal."

"The tail is shattered thoroughly at the base. I was hoping with the X-rays we might be able to give the guy a little more tail, but…" Disappointment spread through her as she got the instruments ready for the amputation.

"Bug won't even notice after it's healed. Dogs are incredibly resilient. Heck, I've heard more than one vet say they are three-legged animals with four legs. Losing his tail is unfortunate but hardly the end of the end of Bug's fun adventures."

She knew that. Beck was saying all the right things. A dog's tail was technically an extension of its spine, but losing it wouldn't do any long-term damage.

"I just thought I might have some good news to deliver. Rather than we had to go farther up so the bobtail I talked to you about is more of a nub." She finished the amputation quickly.

So often in emergency vet medicine it was a tale of we tried this but had to do that. She always hoped for an unexpected "it was smoother than anticipated." Those were so few and far between.

"My dad once worked on an archaeology dig outside the Great Pyramid of Giza."

Violet didn't look up from closing the wound at the base of Bug's now tiny tail. But he had piqued her curiosity. "What? That is so cool."

"Yeah." Beck checked the oxygen mask they had over Bug's snout. "He had pictures that he kept in his office. He always said the pictures made it seem better. That he spent the summer shifting sand and finding nothing."

"Nothing?"

"Nothing. Dad wasn't in a very active dig. To quote him, he was helping to make sure nothing had been missed. And they confirmed that."

"Still. The experience." The old Violet had loved traveling. She'd made a habit of staying over after a competition ended to see the sights. Thomas had never understood, and eventually, she'd stopped.

Another little piece of herself she'd given up to a man who'd never really cared about her.

"You must have traveled to some amazing places with them." She finished up the final stitches, then used a sterile wash to clean the closed wound.

"Nope. They found each other. Settled down in Maine and never looked back. Dad used to say Mom was his greatest adventure."

Beck said the words as if on repetition. Just like she had stories she told over and over. He had the same.

"That is really sweet." To be loved so completely. That was all she'd ever wanted.

"Yes. And boring. They had these great lives, then they met each other, settled down and that was it. They could have had so much more." Beck shrugged. "You ready for me to start waking him?"

"Yes." She stepped back from the table, pulling off her gloves. "Is that why you don't want to marry until you are old? Like thirty-five or so?" She winked hoping to show him she didn't mind the faux pas from the other night.

"Thirty-five isn't old." He didn't look up from Bug as the dog started to come out of the sedation.

The dog would be groggy all day, but animals awoke from sedation much quicker than humans.

"That wasn't an answer to the question." Except it was. She'd heard it the other night in his rule. Violet went over to the sink, washed up and turned to watch Beck finish bringing Bug out of his slumber.

"I just don't want to miss out on anything." He looked over his shoulder. "Like running away to Miami for a weekend with a hottie who wants to make her ex jealous."

She rolled her eyes, then headed for the door. She needed to let Bug's owner know that her boy was doing well, and the tail was going to be very short, but he would 100 percent recover. And she wanted a minute alone too.

Violet wasn't looking to race down the aisle. She was content enough in her town house with Bear. So why was there a tinge of regret brewing in her chest? This was a fling for fun and to save face at the wedding. It wasn't a life jump start.

CHAPTER FIVE

"LET'S GO, TOASTER!" Beck pushed sweat from his eyes as he ran his dog through the course again.

"Now that is the kind of dedication I want to see at this gym." Nancy beamed as she and Oliver stepped onto the agility course.

Beck raised a hand and motioned for Toaster to heel. His girl followed the command, her tail still wagging as they started off on the course. They were competing at regionals as part of the intermediate team. He'd love to say that he was here to make sure Toaster was ready to win, but he didn't care about the prize.

He was running off the emotions he'd created last night when taking care of Bug. Trying to push everything he'd felt for Vi into a cage in the back of his head. Preferably before she got here.

She'd promised him some pointers for Toaster before regionals. An off-handed comment she'd made after Bug's surgery that he'd taken quick advantage of. Again, not for the pointers, but to spend time with Vi.

Something about the way she'd asked if his parents' happy union and settling down was his reason for his *rule one*, made him uncomfortable. Violet hadn't pushed. Hadn't told him it was dumb to avoid marriage after witnessing such a happy union.

That was his college girlfriend's complaint. She'd been furious when they'd gone on a short trip for their one-year anniversary and to celebrate junior year finals and not come back engaged. She'd dumped him about three weeks later. Last he heard she was living in Colorado with her husband and a newborn. He wished her well, but she was the reason he set up rule one.

It was better to be up front about the expectation. That way no one got hurt. His life was full of adventures—the adventures his parents had given up in exchange for vows.

Vi accepted it. She didn't tell him he was a fool for not wanting what they had. So why was this the first time he felt odd about it? It was probably just…well, he didn't know why he was feeling like the rule might be wrong.

The feeling would pass.

"I need to run Oliver through the course. He's slow this week." Nancy pushed past him, Oliver trotting beside her.

He didn't bother to say anything to that. Nancy thought everything was slow except personal records, or PRs. The fact that PRs were rare, that

Oliver was older now, that the course was something he knew so well he might be bored, were not considerations Nancy gave.

In her defense, the woman loved her dog; she just pushed toward prizes that never seemed to come.

"Beck." Violet waved as she stepped through the front door.

Nancy's head snapped. This private training session was about to get an uninvited guest.

"Dr. Lockwood." Nancy ran over, Oliver close at her heels.

"Hi." Vi nodded to Nancy as she stepped beside Beck.

He slid a hand around Violet's waist and kissed the top of her head. The simple motions sent flames down his spine.

Damn.

He had a serious crush on Violet. Getting to touch her, kiss her was igniting his feelings instead of dousing the flames.

"If you are going to be here, you must be a member. I know you came for the potluck as a date, but if you are going to be here for actual gym time…" Nancy put her hands on her hips.

"Members are allowed to sponsor people for a month, Nancy." He'd looked into it following the potluck. Vi had walked away from agility training. She was done with this life, and he had no plans to drag her back in.

"That sponsorship is for people bringing their dogs, Beck. Not trainers." Nancy crossed her arms—she really had the ticked-off owner bit down. "I must be firm, or others might try the same thing."

Lucky for her Vi had no desire to run her own agility gym. Nancy would be out of business to-morrow.

"Of course." Violet smiled.

The look he'd seen on her face at karaoke night was back. The competitor. The winner. Nancy had no idea who she was dealing with.

"Your website, which is outdated, indicates trainers are required to pay the monthly fee plus a sixty percent commission on all lessons." Violet reached into her back pocket, pulling out her phone. "Industry standard is forty percent to the gym."

"Well, I have all the clients here. So they are already gym members." Nancy raised her chin. "I am sure your fees will cover any expenses just fine. You *are* Violet Lockwood."

"I am." She hit a few buttons and held her phone up. An email was clear on the screen. "As you can see, I signed up as a trainer before com-ing in here. For the full year."

Nancy gave a little hop, then caught herself. "Lovely. We are happy to have you. I am sure whatever training schedule you set up will be very fruitful…for you."

It didn't take long for Nancy to see the dollar signs.

"I actually already reached out to the intermediate team. They will be here—" Violet turned her phone around and looked at the clock "—well, any minute, really."

"You are hosting a full training session." Nancy bit her lip, and if he and Vi weren't there, Beck figured she'd dance all the way back to her office.

"Yes. I already worked out the rate with them." Violet grinned, but he knew it was the smile she gave to pet parents she was furious with.

Tim, Lisa and Grace walked in, their dogs, Pickle, Tuna and Posy on leashes by their side. The handlers' grins dropped a little as they looked between Nancy and Violet.

"Hi, guys." Violet was a late-shift ER vet now, but when she'd arrived in Bangor, she'd been a regular shift vet and seen most of the dogs in the gym at some point. "Glad you could make it."

"Wouldn't miss this." Tim rubbed Pickle's ears. The border collie mix had gotten her name after eating nearly half a jar of pickles his daughter had drained and left out, for reasons the then-nine-year-old had not been able to explain.

Pickle had been seen in the office for an upset belly, but the puppy had been fine after a day or so. Tim had gotten her into training as soon as she was doing her business outside.

"Are you sure about the price?" Grace held

on to Posy's leash. The pittie mix loved agility
and was incredibly well trained. People were forever coming up to her, assuming her dog was a
friendly beast.

"I am positive. Go ahead and give it to Nancy."
Vi turned to the owner. "I am going to head out to
the A-frame. Meet me there when you are done."

Nancy didn't bother to hide her glee. "We finally have Violet Lockwood as a trainer."

"I don't think she plans to do this very often."
Lisa pulled a dollar out of her pocket and handed
it to Nancy.

"What is this?"

"Our fee. Violet is doing it for a dollar." Lisa
snapped her fingers and Tuna followed her onto
the agility path.

"A-a d-dollar!" Nancy stuttered as each of the
intermediate team laid a dollar in her hand then
headed onto the field.

Technically, he hadn't worked out a fee with Vi,
but he pulled out a dollar and passed it over too.

Round one to Violet.

"One more lap, everyone. Then we will call it a
night." Violet wrapped her arms around herself
as she watched the intermediate team run along
the outside of the course with their owners.

The dogs had done the course at least twice
but while speed was important, many wins came
down to tuning everything but their owner out

during the competition. Competitions were noisy.
Busy. Filled with a million different scents. It was
a dog's dream and a trainer's nightmare.

"Come on, Oliver." Nancy was racing Oliver
through the course for at least the fifth time.

Violet had not appreciated Nancy's tone when
she came with Beck for the potluck. She'd looked
at the contract for trainers and started steaming.
Beck had said Nancy complained about the lack
of agility trainers at the gym. But she was doing
nothing to court them.

There was a gym in New Port about thirty minutes away. It had two trainers; one she knew lived
in Bangor. But that gym practiced industry stan-
dards of 40 percent for established members of
the gym. If the trainer brought the client in, the
trainer kept 80 percent.

Why would they work at Nancy's gym? Vio-
let didn't plan to really do a lot of training, but it
was the principle.

She blinked. She didn't *plan* to do any training. Tonight was a one-off. She'd explained that
to Tim, Lisa and Grace. A quick hit to get Toaster
fully integrated into the team. Regionals was less
than a month away.

The team might not care if they came away
with trophies, but they needed to be a team. It
was safest for the dogs and their handlers if they
acted as one. Though even with this brief inter-

action it was clear Toaster was going to run with them just fine.

Heck, with a little bit of work they might even place. Not win…though with a lot of work that was not outside the cards. The dogs were all super fit; and most importantly they all loved to run the course. That was one of the biggest indicators of success.

A factor many in the game overlooked. A fast dog only won if it was motivated. You could motivate through routine—not her favorite. Through fear—an absolute nonstarter for her. But nothing motivated an animal like fun.

"You are amazing." Beck wrapped an arm around her shoulders. "Worth so much more than a dollar."

She kissed his cheek. "I appreciate you saying so. I used to charge a hundred dollars an hour."

"Only a hundred?" Beck raised that eyebrow.

"You sound like my ex. He got so upset that I only charged a hundred, unless—" She bit her lip and cleared her throat.

"Unless?" Beck squeezed her shoulder as they started toward the locker area.

"Unless it was clear they were only there for me personally." She let out an involuntary shake. "Thomas used to plaster my face all over our social media sites. He bragged that my beauty drove so much business."

It was creepy. But more, it was infuriating; it

diminished her talent. Most of her clients came to her because they wanted *her* to train their dogs so that they won. Not because she was a pretty face.

Thomas had huffed more than once about her unwillingness to wear a full face of makeup with her hair done while she was training. He had not understood her reasons about comfort and heat—or more likely he just hadn't liked them. With time—and some therapy—she'd finally concluded he liked the idea of her more than her.

"I take it some of the men who showed up weren't interested in agility." Beck didn't even bother to make that sound like a question.

"A few showed up without a dog. I actually took one guy's money. I told him it was three hundred an hour that time, and then ran him through the course for an hour and a half. He was not pleased."

"Why didn't he just leave?"

Violet let out a laugh that she knew had no humor. "Because then he would have had to admit that he was there to try to sleep with me."

Beck leaned against the lockers, letting his hand graze Toaster's head. "And your at-the-time-fiancé didn't bother to step in? He was a trainer. He could have run the session or sent the guy packing."

He could have. But Thomas was more excited that because he'd stayed for the extra thirty minutes, that meant they got to charge him six hundred dollars. That was the night she should have walked away from her engagement. Should have packed her things or better yet, packed his and kicked him to the curb.

But she'd believed in fairy tales then. Had wanted the fairy tale so bad. Still did. But that want was never going to blind her again.

"It wasn't his style." She knew the words were clipped; knew Beck knew too.

His head bounced back just a hair, but the smile never faded. His dimples were certainly easy to look at.

"Why don't we stop for coffee? We can get Toaster a pup cup. She has certainly earned it." Beck pushed off the locker and offered her a hand. "My treat since you refused to take an actual paycheck for training the team tonight. But you have to admit one thing."

His dimples deepened. If she was ever going to swoon it was over dimples like his.

"What?"

"You had fun tonight."

"Of course." Vi wrapped her arm through his elbow. "You are very fun to be around, Beck."

"I am." He dropped a kiss on her forehead.

"And so modest." She playfully hit his hip with hers. "Modesty is certainly one of your top characteristics."

"So glad you see that. But I wasn't talking about fun with me."

Her steps didn't falter but her heart dropped. That last line stung. She'd had fun *with* him.

"You enjoyed being back on the course. Enjoyed the agility work. I know Bear has no desire to run a course but you—you like being here."

No. She loved being at the agility gym. Violet drank in the energy the owners got from racing through obstacles. She came alive when a pup jumped in its owner's arms at the end, tail wagging. Knowing it was the bestest girl or boy in that moment.

But this was part of her past.

It doesn't have to be.

Her chest tightened as they headed to the exit. She'd joined. Yes, to prove a point to Nancy. But she was a member…and a trainer…for a year. She could come back anytime.

Violet had to do her best not to turn and look back before the door closed.

CHAPTER SIX

THE CLOCK WAS ticking down. Twenty-four hours before they landed in Miami. Did they know enough? Was the rouse going to work? They still had enough time to call it off. Enough time for her to own up to Fiona that she and Beck weren't a real couple.

Sure they'd been on a coffee date and to a karaoke bar. But could you really call training, coffee, and bad singing with a kiss in the parking lot dating?

No.

And the kiss. He hadn't kissed her after their coffee date. Hadn't asked if he could. Hadn't brought it up at all.

That shouldn't bother her. It didn't bother her.

Sure, Vi. You keep telling yourself that.

Her phone pinged.

The pic Fiona sent of herself next to a dress bag holding her wedding gown with a thumbs-up and a glass of champagne sped up the ticking of the clock in her head. Twenty-four hours!

Before Violet could respond, another text popped in.

Can't wait to meet your boyfriend. You haven't even sent me a picture. The text ended with a frowny face emoji.

Violet looked up to where Beck was looking over some results on the computer. She bit her lip, then snapped a quick photo.

Pulling it into the chat, she hesitated. "Beck."

He looked up, pushing his glasses up his nose a little. Damn. That was the photo she should have gotten. Hot vet tech with glasses. Real, nerdy, hottie aura going on.

Heat raced across her skin. Man, she'd never thought she had a type, but...

"Did you need something, Vi?"

"Yes. Sorry." She'd gotten lost in her own thoughts. Of him. "Fiona is texting."

"Getting cold feet?"

The question hovered between them.

"Nope. She loves Patrick. They could have gotten hitched at a busted-up courthouse, with no one they knew watching, and she'd have been on cloud nine to be his wife." That was another red flag she'd missed.

Thomas had wanted a fancy wedding. He'd insisted on having a top caterer. The best photographer they could afford. The demands were ironic considering he'd seen none of it, but they'd had to pay for everything.

"That is the way it should be. My parents were married at the courthouse as soon as they got back to the States. My dad used to joke that his parents found out about my mom the day after they'd made everything legal." Beck's eyes closed for a moment as he clearly relived a happy time.

It was weird how he was so insistent on putting marriage off when he'd come from a happy home. She'd come from the exact opposite and had wanted the union so badly.

"She wants a photo of you. I snapped one while you were looking at Pi's results. I was going to just send it but that felt like such an invasion of privacy and…" Her words seemed to run off.

"Let me see it." Beck stepped up and looked at the photo. He was bending over and you could see the pensive look on his face, his glasses just a little down his nose.

"You captured my best side."

"What?"

"My backside. I've heard my butt is quite delicious." Beck crossed his arms, giving her a look full of glee.

If she said it wasn't his best side it would be a lie. If she said it was, she admitted to focusing on his butt.

"I thought you said your right side was your best side? You were very insistent as I recall." She pursed her lips to keep the laughter in.

Beck's dimples popped out, and she mentally snapped that picture. "Touché."

"But that isn't the photo you should send." He pulled his phone out of his pocket.

It took a second, but her phone dinged and she looked at the adorable photo of him and Toaster at the agility park. It was perfection.

She quickly forwarded it to Fiona, then bit her lip. "Care to take a selfie of us to send, too?"

"You bet!" He wrapped an arm around her shoulders, his dimples showing so perfectly in the photo.

Violet snapped the photo and sent the picture off. "So, do Pi's results show a skin infection?" She already knew the answer. Or rather she was 90 percent certain she knew.

"No." Beck blew out a breath. The fun demeanor shifting away in an instant. "No mites. No bacteria. No fungus. Perfect skin."

Which meant the herding dog was pulling out his fur because of OCD. It was something she'd seen before. It was more common in working dogs, but any dog could develop it.

"Did Margery mention how long it's been since Pi's been in the field?" Margery ran a sheep farm, but the Australian cattle dog had been out of commission due to a foot injury for at least a month.

Every dog had a purpose. Her Bear's purpose was to laze around, give snuggles, eat as much as possible and fart at the most inopportune moments. A cattle dog's main purpose was to herd cattle.

She'd seen herding dogs who needed to retire because of age or injury who adjusted to live as a house pet easily…or semi-easily. Often, they took to herding other animals in the house or the children.

Other herders never adjusted to a new life.

"All right, let's go talk to Margery." Violet took a deep breath. In many ways the best answer would have been mites, or even a hard-to-treat fungal infection. Mental health issues were hard enough to treat in humans where you could have an actual conversation. In animals, it could be a lifelong challenge.

Pi was pacing the room as they walked into the small suite where Margery was waiting. The older woman was holding her arms as she stared at Pi. Tears ran down her cheeks as she looked over at Violet and Beck.

"It's OCD, isn't it? Not a fungal infection or mites." She ran the back of her hand over her cheeks.

Some people had a misconception that people who had working dogs didn't care about them as much as people whose dogs' whole purpose was just to love them. It wasn't true.

"Yes." Violet set her tablet chart on the counter and stepped over to Margery as she let out a sob.

"Pi stepped on a rock three weeks ago. He saw

Dr. Brown who diagnosed a sprained tendon. Pi needs rest, but he won't accept it. But he is still favoring that back left leg. If I let him herd the sheep, he might tear the tendon. If I don't, he paces nonstop in the house." Margery let out a sob as she watched Pi continue to circle the room.

"I've got food puzzles and interactive play toys but…" She shrugged. "He isn't interested in any of that."

That wasn't a surprise. Cattle dogs were bred to herd. It was an instinct. She often warned new pet parents that you could train a dog, and you should, but you couldn't train the innate breed characteristics out of them.

"I think our best option is to get Pi on a low dose of serotonin reuptake inhibitors."

"You mean SSRIs?" Margery bit her lip as she watched Pi continue his rounds. "I am on a low dose of Prozac for anxiety and seasonal affective disorder."

"Yes. I mean SSRIs. Sometimes, just like with humans, the brain needs a little help. Once Pi gets back into the field the symptoms will probably subside, but you should come back during regular business hours to see Dr. Brown if they don't."

"Probably won't." Margery gave her a watery smile. "I know I pay an upcharge for after-hours emergency care but getting here during regular hours hardly ever works out. And Pi likes you." She double clicked the training clicker she had in her hand. Pi came, sitting at her feet before looking up at her.

The dog was focused. Too focused.

"All right. I will get the prescription written up and our in-house pharmacy can fill it. I want to warn you that SSRIs take time to build up in the system. You won't see the full effect from them for a month. But I want you to follow up after six weeks."

"If Pi is not back in the field by then, both of us will be beside ourselves." Margery rubbed the dog's ears.

"Understandable." Beck turned to grab some of the patient education materials they kept in the cabinet.

As she headed through the door to the back of the clinic, she heard him carefully going over the medication and then offering some of his own tricks for dealing with a dog with high drive needs.

The man was born to work in this field.

"Why the frown?" Beck had taken too much pleasure in Vi sending a pic of them to her friend. This was a fun fling. They were enjoying dates, and they'd shared a few kisses. There was hardly a significant reason for his heart to have floated when he looked at the selfie of them she'd sent to Fiona.

"Oh." Violet looked up from her phone. "Fiona says we make a great couple."

He barely kept the frown off his face. This was what she wanted. What they were attempting to accomplish. Why was she upset that it was working?

And why am I upset that she isn't thrilled at the idea of her friend thinking we are great couple?

That was a worry for another day.

"She thinks we make a great couple from a photo. And I mean... I am so glad you agreed to this, but now that we are taking off tomorrow morning... I... I..."

Rose coated her cheeks as she failed to find any words.

"Now you worry we are going to fall flat on our faces?"

"Yes." She looked relieved that he'd said what she was struggling to vocalizing. They'd worked together for two years, but he'd always been able to fill in the blanks with Vi. It was a weird superpower that he'd joked about with the other vet techs only once.

He could still see their faces as he talked about how easy it was to read her. How he could finish her sentences because she was an open book. The other vet techs had each shaken their heads and informed him that he was out of his mind.

Bethany, a vet tech who'd left the practice about six months ago, had flat out asked if he was sleeping with her. Because none of them could read Vi's mind. In fact, she worried constantly that Dr.

Lockwood was mad at her because the woman was so quiet.

He'd clammed up quickly after that. Never sharing how easy it was for him around Vi. At least now that weird superpower came in handy.

"We have been on three dates. Everyone knows that if you make it to date four then things have a chance to get serious." Vi put her phone in her scrub pocket and headed over to where they were running tests on a puppy that had come in with what the owner swore was parvo, a devastating and highly fatal disease for puppies.

The rapid test had come back negative, and Violet was certain it wasn't parvo. But the patient's owner had insisted on the additional test.

"Everyone knows that? I thought it was the third date people chat about." As soon as the words were out, his face heated.

"That's just because so many people say they wait until the third date to sleep with someone. But I mean that isn't really that big of a deal. It's the fourth date, the one that can no longer be called 'testing' for a relationship that matters." Vi said the words with such ease.

His mouth was hanging open. Beck knew that. Knew that his brain was misfiring.

"And we haven't had that fourth date. We are asking people to believe we've been together six months and we haven't had a fourth date. I mean, I think people are going to suspect."

He wanted to say, so what if they do. It was how he really felt. They were people she rarely saw. Fiona wouldn't care. But if Vi cared, then he wanted this to work for her.

"How about we do our fourth date tomorrow morning?"

"That's sweet." She looked up from the lab work she was running on the puppy. "But we are supposed to be at the airport so early—at least when you work the late shift you don't have to worry too much about oversleeping the alarm."

So true. He actually planned to stay awake until they got on the plane, then catch some shut-eye.

"There are coffee shops in the airport. Let's get there, have a fourth date."

"Great. We can get into the nitty-gritty of what we want out of relationships and the future."

Luckily her head was bent over the test results so she didn't see him take a step back as those words hit him. He was getting into dangerous water here. Sure they'd shared kisses and had laughs together, but he'd been very clear that he had no intention of marrying and Vi… Vi wanted marriage.

Maybe she didn't say it. But one did not get that close to the altar with a walking red flag unless you wanted the fairy tale. He couldn't give it to her. But maybe he could help her practice so she was ready when the opportunity presented itself.

"Yeah." The word felt so hollow but he forced it

out. "Yeah, that is exactly what I mean. So, fourth date at the airport coffee shop."

"That actually sounds pretty romantic." Vi met his gaze. "Good news. No parvo. Bad news, we don't know why Tofu is so lethargic."

She crossed her arms as she leaned against the counter. "Pluses, no blood in the stool, no parasites and the lethargy isn't terrible—yet." Violet took a deep breath. "Negatives, vomiting, diarrhea and Tofu was the runt of the litter. Mom has had little interaction with the guy, and Billy's daughter is supplementing feeding."

"What is his daughter supplementing with?" Alarm bells were going off in Beck's head.

"Billy says he bought canned puppy formula so I assume that." Vi tilted her head. "What are you thinking?"

"When I was in school, we had a puppy present with similar digestive issues. The owner was giving the puppy cow's milk as a substitute for the mother not making enough for the litter of seven she had. It caused severe digestion issues."

"But if they have canned puppy supplement?" Vi shook her head. "I can't imagine why they would also use cow's milk."

"Billy's daughter is a teen. Sometimes they do things that don't make sense. This is a long shot, but there are no parasites and the parvo is negative. Our puppy got so sick, its kidneys shut down before the vet figured out what was going on.

The little guy is a big guy now and doing fine last I heard, but it was touch and go for a while." Maybe he was barking up the wrong tree but this was plausible.

And they had nothing else to go on.

"Let's ask." Vi grabbed the test results she knew Billy would want to see and headed toward the door.

"It's not parvo."

Beck was always impressed that Violet didn't wait to deliver good or bad news. He enjoyed working with Dr. Brown, but the man tried to lay the groundwork for each diagnosis. It was his way of being helpful, but Beck had seen more than one pet parent start to panic as they waited for the actual results.

Billy rubbed Tofu's ears but a tear slipped down his cheek. "I'm glad but then what? Because Tofu is tiny but mighty. She hasn't let being the runt slow her down at all."

"Is there any chance someone in your house is giving her cow's milk?" It was a gentle way to ask the question, but there was authority behind it.

"Cow's milk?" Billy squeezed his eyes shut. "Like from the grocery store cow's milk?" He opened his eyes. "Sorry. Dumb question I know."

"No. I know this is a unique ask." Violet offered a small smile.

Billy reached into his pocket and pulled out a

cell. He put it on a speaker as it started to ring. It took a moment, but finally his daughter answered.

"Daddy? Is Tofu all right? Does she have parvo?"

"Alex, take a deep breath. No, she doesn't have parvo, but Dr. Lockwood is worried she might have gotten some cow's milk."

"Oh." The line went quiet, and all the adults in the room looked at each other.

"How much milk have you given Tofu?" Violet's words were soft, as she leaned over the phone. Not giving Billy's daughter a chance to shift her story was a good option. It wasn't that kids lied, it was that they often tried to make excuses and the webs spun into more and more, before they finally admitted the truth.

"The puppy milk cans were in the basement, and I was running late for school." She let out a cry on the other end of the phone.

"Alex!"

Vi held up her hand as Billy raised his voice. There was time for him to discipline and explain what consequences could happen, but right now they needed answers. It was amazing to watch this woman work.

"How much, Alex? I need to know so we can treat Tofu best."

A whimper carried across the line. "I have used it in the morning before school the last four days. But at night I was using puppy milk. I was."

"It never dawned on you to bring a can up from the basement at night when you went down…" Billy sucked in a deep breath.

"Did I kill Tofu?"

"No."

"No."

"No."

All three adults answered at the same time and Tofu lifted her head, gave her tail a tiny wag.

"We'll talk about this when I get home, Alex. But Tofu is going to be okay." Billy told his daughter he loved her, then hung up.

"The good news is digestive distress is much easier to treat than parvo. I am going to prescribe something to calm her stomach and let her rest for the next several days. Schedule a regular checkup for Monday or Tuesday with Dr. Brown. And give her lots of love."

"Thanks, Dr. Lockwood."

Violet headed through the door to the back and he followed.

"Nice work." She smiled as she grabbed the chart and filled out the information for the prescription. "I would never have asked about cow's milk."

"Glad to have helped. My parents would have grounded me for a month if I pulled something like that. I suspect Alex will get something similar."

"She's lucky Billy isn't the type to give away

her dog like my mom would have." She shrugged lightly in a way that broke his heart. Did she really understand how sad her childhood had been? Sometimes he wondered.

Violet opened her mouth, but before she could say anything else, the three dings echoed again.

Another emergency. Damn!

CHAPTER SEVEN

BECK YAWNED AS he stood behind Violet in the security line at the airport. The sun wouldn't cross the horizon for a couple more hours, and he hadn't managed to get any shut-eye last night. The emergency had been a house fire.

The pup, Hemingway, had burns on his tail and was dealing with smoke inhalation. His kitty friend, Ben, had been found an hour later, severe burns on her paws. Both cuties were going to be okay, but it had made for an extremely long shift.

That was not going to derail him though. Exhaustion was a choice, and he planned to look as upbeat and excited as possible for this "fourth date."

She slipped her shoes off, and he grinned at her socks.

Violet followed his gaze and stretched her toes. "I found a place that puts anything you want on a pair of socks."

"And Bear's face is almost the perfect choice."

Vi's mouth opened, clearly ready to argue about

the *almost perfect* words, but he reached down and yanked his tennis shoes off.

"Oh my gosh." Vi pointed at Toaster's face.

"Toaster *is* the best thing you can put on socks."

Violet put her hands on her hips and shook her head. "On that we will have to agree to disagree but—" she pointed to their feet "—great minds think alike."

They certainly seemed to. Matching animal socks was very couple-like. Even if they hadn't meant too.

He pushed their carry-on luggage forward and stood back while she headed through security. Then he followed.

"I can't believe you have Toaster on your socks." Vi chuckled as she slid the bright pink slip-on shoes back on.

"Why not? You have Bear on yours." He'd gotten the socks as a Christmas present last year. Although could you really call it a present if you bought all the gifts yourself?

He'd been alone for the holidays for two years now. His father had passed when he was a freshman in college. His mother had followed two years ago, though the dementia had stolen her before that.

It was weird to be alone so young, but he still made the cookies his father loved and stuffed his stocking for his mother. It was a little way to stay connected to his family.

"True. But most men probably wouldn't wear them or, if they did, they'd wear them at home."

Beck didn't know about that. He had several male friends he was sure would put their pets on socks. Hell, Marcus had a special hoody so his cat could be carried. It was the only way he managed to get anything done since the animal was so clingy.

"That is their loss. If a man let what others thought of him stop him from doing something he wanted to do, then he had no one to blame but himself. I actually have Toaster on three pairs of socks. I got a deal if I ordered more than two pairs." He grabbed their bags and pointed toward the coffee shop.

Then stopped and frowned. The lineup appeared to be never-ending. It seemed everyone on the first flight of the day was stopping here before heading to their gates.

The few seats the coffee shop had were already claimed. Well, they could take their coffee to the gate.

"Ugh." Vi looked at the line. "I think this is the universe's way of telling me no caffeine, so maybe there is some hope that I'll sleep on the trip down even though I'm stuck in a middle seat."

"Middle seat?" Beck wanted to kick himself. He'd meant to make sure they had two seats together. Even the high of going on an adventure was not enough to kick his brain into gear when he was so exhausted.

Vi had been stoic through all their cases last night, but he knew it weighed on her. Sometimes working in the veterinarian world simply sucked. There were no other words for it.

"Yeah. The only thing left on the flight are two seats in first class. So middle seat, here I come." She yawned, then hung her head a bit. "Sorry, I'm not the best travel companion right now."

It was five fifty in the morning. They'd worked a tough shift and had an early morning flight, with a connection in DC before reaching Miami. Now she was apologizing for not being what— perky?

Reaching over, he wrapped an arm around her shoulders. "I think you are an excellent travel partner. Let's go to the gate and just relax. I think we earned it after that shift."

Leaning her head against his shoulder, Violet let out a soft sigh. "It was rough. But today is a new day."

When they got to the gate, he set his bags next to hers, then made a quick excuse and headed to talk to the gate agent. With any luck, he could see about those two first class tickets or at least get her moved into first class.

"Good morning." Beck smiled at the gate agent.

"How can I help you?" The young man took a

deep breath and put a smile on his face, but Beck could see the hesitation.

Airport brought out the worst in some people. During his travels he'd seen more than one inexcusable attack on the gate agents who were just trying to do their jobs. "I'm heading to Miami for a wedding. My girlfriend is a bridesmaid. We purchased tickets separately, and she is stuck in a middle seat."

"The flight is sold out, except for two first class seats. I'm sorry, sir."

"I know. But I was wondering if I could use my points to upgrade us to first class, or just her, if I don't have enough. She's an emergency veterinarian. Last night's shift was a hard one, and I just want her to rest before she has to dive into wedding stuff for her friend."

The man looked over to where Violet stood waiting, then back at Beck. "You would be fine with her being in first class but not you?"

Beck waited for a moment. Was there more to that question? "I'm sorry. It's early and I haven't had any caffeine so I don't really understand the question. Of course, it's fine if only she can sit up there."

The man let out a soft chuckle. "I had a guy yesterday who bumped himself from a middle seat and left his wife, three-month-old and six-year-old in coach."

"What!" That was horrific.

"Exactly." The man rolled his eyes. "The things you see. Can I have your names?"

Beck provided them, and the attendant tapped out a few quick things on his keyboard. Beck's phone dinged once, then again.

The attendant smiled. "You're both in first class on both flights."

"Both? I don't think I have enough points for both flights. Can you just make it her all the way down?"

The attendant shook his head. "Nope. I didn't use the points. I can upgrade at the gate for all sorts of reasons, and it's nice to have someone just be kind for a change. Have a great trip, sir."

"Thank you." He turned and headed back to Vi.

She was already holding up her phone as he took the seat next to her. "What magic did you just pull? First class on both flights!"

"No magic. I just asked if I could use my points."

"No. No. You are already doing so much, Beck. I can't ask you to use your points too."

Wrapping his arm around her shoulders, he kissed her forehead. Why couldn't he stop the little touches? A fling was fun—and he'd had more than one in the past few years. Women who'd he'd hung out with for a few months, enjoying their time together. But he'd never found himself reaching for them without thinking. Dropping little kisses here and there.

At least it would look more natural at the wedding if they acted this way.

"You didn't ask. I acted. And it doesn't matter because the agent had a real louse of a guy yesterday and more than a few irate customers over the course of his career, so just being nice before six in the morning was enough." He looked at his watch, debating if there was enough time for a coffee run.

Violet laid her head against his shoulder, and all thoughts of seeking out coffee disappeared. No drink was worth giving this up.

"Guess our coffee date is off then." Vi yawned and snuggled against his shoulder.

"We can still have it. Just here." He leaned his head against hers. His eyes were heavy but he didn't dare close them. "So, Miami. You exchanged sun and heat for Bangor's less sunny much colder climate. Think you will head back south eventually?"

Every once in a while he searched on the real-estate apps for property and for a moment considered selling the house and trying someplace new. But the memories of his parents; the happiness he'd had there. He wasn't ready to give the link to his parents up.

At least not yet.

"No." Vi giggled. "Don't tell that to any of my friends at the wedding. They won't believe you.

I think the idea that anyone would trade in the sand and sun for snow and gray-filled winters is beyond them."

She wasn't planning to leave Bangor. That made him oddly happy.

"I don't think our winters are really gray." Beck had heard more than one person comment about how Maine was gorgeous in three seasons but that didn't override the bleakness of the fourth.

"They aren't."

He smiled at Vi's simple words.

"They are frozen, but there is a beauty that comes with first snowfall. It's a season for hibernation and relaxing and staying warm with friends." She let out another yawn. "There is no way I can stay awake on the first flight. I think the first-class amenities will be an absolute waste on me."

Beck yawned, too. "We will be able to stretch out—at least as much as one can on an airplane. Not a waste."

"Not a great date, either." Violet turned, her dark eyes holding his.

"It's unique. That's the definition of great in my opinion."

She pressed a kiss against his cheek. "You are too perfect."

"Good. That will mean we'll make a great impression at the wedding."

* * *

"What do you think?" Beck stepped out of the hotel bathroom dressed in a light brown linen suit with a dark mocha shirt underneath.

Damn.

Violet had to swallow the rush of desire as she stared at his perfection. They'd slept on both flights down. She was still a little tired, but Beck looked like he was fully recharged…and ready to go. "That suit looks lovely on you."

If the suit looked that delicious on him, she couldn't wait to see the tux on Beck's muscular form.

"Well, I have to keep up with my date." He gestured to her. "You look gorgeous. Drop-dead gorgeous."

Beck tilted his head in such an approving look that she felt her toes curl in the taupe high heels she'd chosen for the floral minidress. It was the first time she'd worn the dress she'd found in a boutique downtown. It came to the top of her thighs, had long sleeves and a high neck, and was covered in dozens of different flowers. It was colorful and sexy as hell.

She loved it the second she saw it on the mannequin. Loved it more when she stood in front of the mirror in the dressing room. It had taken her over a year to have a reason to wear it, but it was worth it to see the look on Beck's face.

"Thank you." She'd sent a picture of herself

to Fiona in the dress. It showed off Violet's long legs. It was a statement piece, but this wasn't her wedding. She wanted to make sure she approved. Fiona had sent back that if Violet didn't wear it to the rehearsal, she'd take it as a personal affront.

Beck held out his elbow. They were meeting the rest of the wedding party in the hotel lobby to take the party bus to the Frost Museum of Science. "Ready?"

"Yes." She smiled up at him. It was nice having him here. Yes, they were playing a game, but Beck was fun to be around. He called her Vi and laughed with her. He paid attention and cared about people.

And he kissed like an absolute god.

She was getting ready to support Fiona as her bridesmaid and friend. But she was also about to see the man she'd foolishly expected to spend the rest of her life with. She should feel more nervous about that, but on Beck's arm it was impossible to feel self-conscious.

Her heels put her at the perfect height to place a kiss on his cheek. He'd held her in the airport. Kissed her forehead several times. It should feel weird to kiss him. Awkward to share the little touches partners did without thinking.

Instead it felt oddly…right.

Violet wasn't sure what to do with that, but that was a problem for future Violet. This weekend was going to be fun. Period.

They headed to the elevator bank, and all the good vibes they'd had seemed to get sucked out of the universe as she came face-to-face with a woman who looked remarkably like her.

"Wow." Beck blew out a breath.

He pulled her a little closer as the woman she knew must be Thomas's wife stared at her. The woman's hair was a shade lighter, her features a little softer than Violet's but the resemblance was uncanny.

She was wearing a knee-length yellow dress with a deep décolletage, paired with a teardrop amethyst necklace. One identical to the piece Thomas had given her for their first anniversary.

Cringe thy name is Thomas.

Awkward did not begin to describe the interaction as the two stared at each other.

"You have a doppelgänger." Beck chuckled but she could see him look above the elevator, probably hoping it would arrive so that whatever was going on ended quicker.

Unfortunately Violet knew the woman was getting on the party bus with them. The only saving grace was that Thomas wasn't with her.

"You must be Violet."

She smiled, grateful that Beck pulled her a little closer. He might not know exactly what was going on, but the man could read a room.

"I am. I apologize, but I don't know your name."

The woman lifted her hand, fingering the tear-drop necklace. "Mrs. Dove Lowerly."

"It's nice to meet you." The waves of emotion she'd expected failed to crest. Maybe she would get through this weekend unscathed.

"Violet."

Nope. Her body tensed, and Beck squeezed her waist again as Thomas stepped around them and next to his bride.

"Hi, honey." He pressed his lips to Dove's. The motion was not gentle. It lacked love—in her opinion.

He'd done the same thing to her when he wanted people to understand she was with him. One of the red flags she'd ignored. Now he was doing the same to Dove.

Fury pulled at her, but Dove wrapped her arms around Thomas's neck, leaning into the possessive intent. If she was unbothered by the domineering attitude, then it wasn't Violet's place to interfere.

The elevator finally arrived. Thomas and Dove stepped in. Beck hugged her gently as they stepped in.

"So who are you?" Thomas started as soon as the door closed. His eyes were trained on Beck. It was a look he'd give competitors on the agility course.

It wasn't appropriate there and it certainly wasn't appropriate here.

"Beck Forester." He kissed her head. "And you?"

Thomas let out a slow chuckle. "I think you know who I am."

Beck tilted his head, looked at her, then shrugged. "Sorry. No. Should I?"

Violet turned her head into Beck's shoulder, glad she had a matte, no-smear lipstick on because there was no way to keep herself from laughing if she had to look at Thomas. And Beck's suit was too perfect to ruin with bright red lipstick.

He was sputtering. And she knew from standing at his side for far too long that his cheeks were going from pale to fire-engine red. It was something he hated about himself but couldn't control.

"Thomas Lowerly." The words were curt. Spit out. "I am sure *that* clears it up."

"Sorry, it doesn't ring a bell. Are you old friends?"

The elevator door opened before Thomas could say anything else. She could not have scripted a better first meeting with Thomas.

"Come on. I have to introduce you to Fiona. She is going to love you." Violet kissed Beck's cheek, then pulled him out of the elevator.

This was a new experience, and she was going to enjoy every minute.

"So how did you and *Violet* meet?" Thomas crossed his arms as he stood next to Beck.

The groomsmen were lining up for the rehearsal. Beck had hoped the man would avoid him and Violet after the uncomfortable elevator ride. Apparently not.

"Vi and I work together."

"You don't look old enough to be a vet."

"I'm not a vet. I'm a vet tech specialist." He ignored the smirk on Thomas's face. He'd gotten his degree, then a specialty license in emergency and critical care. He was very content with the career he'd chosen.

"But not a doctor of veterinarian medicine." It wasn't a question. It was clear from the glee on Thomas's face that he was happy Beck was "only" a vet tech.

His parents had doctoral degrees in their chosen fields, and they'd often reminded him that it just meant they'd spent more years in school and focused on something very specific. It didn't mean they were better than anyone else that they got to have "Dr." in front of their names.

"Are you a doctor?" Beck didn't actually care, but he took a little too much satisfaction in seeing the man's smirk fall away.

"No. Trainer. And business owner." He cleared his throat as the music started.

Violet was standing at the front of the procession, a bouquet of paper flowers in her hands. She was smiling and took a moment to find him. She offered a saucy little wink and Beck chuckled.

"She do any training in Bangor?" Thomas's question was low and barely audible.

Beck wanted to pretend not to hear it, but the man beside him was certainly capable of starting a scene. This was Fiona and her fiancé's night. A fact that should be easy for Thomas to understand as the stepbrother of the groom.

"Not really. She is focused on emergency medicine." The one practically free training lesson she'd given the intermediate team wasn't much. She'd had fun. So much fun, but her focus was her veterinary practice. That made sense; Vi had worked hard to become a vet.

He looked around wondering if there was a way to move to another seat. Not without turning a few heads. So he stayed where he was.

Luckily, the man seemed content to keep his mouth shut for the rest of the short ceremony. As soon as Violet walked down the aisle on the arm of a groomsman as the last bridesmaid to leave, Beck stepped around Thomas and followed his date.

He had no intention of fueling any discussion with the man. He was here for Vi. And she was getting what she wanted this weekend. So he'd deal with the nosy ex, but only when he had to.

"Isn't this venue amazing?" Violet's eyes lit up as she looked at the tank of jellyfish floating next to them.

"Yeah. I've never seen a wedding and reception in a museum before." When the party bus had pulled up to the Frost Museum of Science, Beck had looked around to see if there was some other venue he was missing, but no. The bride and groom were getting married under a thirty-plus-foot oculus with sharks and schools of colorful fish swimming by. Then the reception was going to be in The Deep, an aquarium area that was filled with tanks and portholes.

It was unique and fun but standing next to Vi was the best part of this adventure.

"Fiona has an aquatic medicine certificate, and Patrick is a marine biologist focused on conservation efforts. The two of them make the perfect team. Look." She held up the bouquet she'd used at the rehearsal.

It was paper flowers with marine life on them. "Wait, are those—"

"Yep. Fiona took the brochures people put in the recycle bin at the exit of the science museum and made all of our bouquets out of them. We are supposed to give them to her so she can compost them."

"Impressive." He'd never thought much about marriage. The few friends he'd seen tie the knot had all settled down into quiet married life. There were even babies starting to arrive now.

It was sweet, but at twenty-six, he wasn't ready to settle into a quiet matrimonial life. His parents had traveled the world, had experiences documented in large photo albums that he'd thumbed through so often they were cemented in his memory.

And every single one of those fun moments had ended right after they'd said their vows. He didn't doubt they'd been happy, but it was like they'd closed a chapter of their lives when they married. A chapter he was not ready to seal shut.

"Yeah. She is so much fun. Now it is dinner and dancing time. You up for it?"

She hit his hip with hers. It seemed to be something she did without thinking, a little touch for fun.

He liked it. A lot.

Pulling her close, he ran a thumb down her cheek, then pressed a featherlight kiss to her lips. They were supposed to be boyfriend and girlfriend after all. "I'm up for anything with you."

Color bloomed on Vi's cheeks, and she looked down as she shook her head. "Anything covers a lot."

"It sure does."

"You make her glow. I haven't seen that...ever." Fiona held out a drink to him as she looked out at the rest of the rehearsal dinner guests.

"I think it's the bride who is supposed to glow." Beck took the drink she offered and raised it toward her. "And you do. Congratulations."

"Thank you." Fiona grinned, but the look in her eye gave him a moment's pause. "But we aren't talking about me."

"It's the night before your wedding." One of Beck's friends had ended an engagement with a woman because she was so focused on the wedding, he'd feared she had no interest in the life that came after. A proven concern when she walked down the aisle not even a year later and filed divorce papers before the first anniversary.

Most brides weren't focused only on the wedding, but the night before they walked down the aisle it was, understandably, their primary concern.

"We have our marriage license and an officiant approved to sign said license in the State of Florida. After tomorrow I'll be Patrick's wife. Everything else is just icing on the cake."

Fiona took a sip of her drink never letting her eyes leave his. "But what I want to talk about right now, before Violet gets back from the bathroom, is you."

Beck let out an uncomfortable chuckle. "Is this where you tell me if I hurt her, you'll hunt me down?"

The bride tilted her head. "Do you need me to tell you that? Are you planning to hurt her?"

"Of course not!" Maybe the words were said too fast for someone who'd offered to pretend to be a long-term boyfriend but only offered a fling.

That didn't change the facts. He had no intention of hurting Violet. Period.

They were having fun.

"Good." Fiona raised a brow as she took another drink.

She didn't say anything else, didn't ask how they'd met or how long they'd been dating. If he had to make a guess, she understood exactly how long he'd been in the picture.

"Fiona." Violet was smiling as she joined them, but her focus was directed completely on the bride. "Are you keeping Beck company?"

"Yes. We were just getting to know each other." Fiona shrugged as she looked at him, a dare in her eye for him to offer any kind of disagreement.

She leaned over and kissed Violet's cheek. "I need to see to a few more of the guests. But no one is using the dance floor. I know how much you like dancing."

"You do?" Those were the wrong words.

Fiona let out a giggle and shook her head as she walked away. "She does."

"I don't think she buys our story. I'm sorry, Vi."

She looked over at the dance floor, then back at him. "I don't think Fiona was ever going to buy this. But I'm glad you're here, whether anyone believes this—" she gestured between them "—or not."

"Want to dance?" He set his drink on the high table next to him and held out her hand.

Violet beamed as she put her hand in his. "Hell yeah!"

They scooted out onto the dance floor, his hand holding hers up in the air. She was already swishing to the beat as he pulled her around to face him.

The blue lights of the aquarium tanks softened everything around them. No one else was on the dance floor, and even if there was, there was no way he could look away from the siren in front of him.

"Do you dance much?" Vi put his hand on her waist as they, or rather she, moved instinctively to the beat. He just did his best to follow the lead she was setting.

"No." He grinned as she wrapped her arms around his neck, her hips brushing against his. "All of my limited musical talents were on show when we sang the 'Monster Mash.'"

"Relax." She shifted in his arms.

He wasn't sure that was possible when the beauty before him was sending all sorts of thoughts through his mind with her movements.

She turned, so her butt was pressed against him, laughing as Fiona, Patrick and several other guests joined them on the floor. For the next twenty minutes, he lost track of everything except for the feel of her against him, the beat of the music and the happiness flowing through him.

"All right folks!" The DJ called out as the fast song softened into a slow ballad. "The bride and groom and all of the wedding party need to get going. Big day tomorrow and I will be here to rock these tunes. But let's set the right mood for the final dance."

A love song started to play. The couples around them pulled each other close. Beck didn't hesitate.

Vi's soft arms went around his neck. "Thank you for dancing with me." She sighed as she laid her head his shoulder.

He pressed his lips to the top of her head. "Of course."

"It was nice to have a dance partner." She kissed his cheek.

It was a sad statement but given that Thomas had not stepped onto the dance floor with his partner, it didn't surprise him. "I will be your dance partner anytime you want."

It was promise he wasn't really in a position to make. When they got back to Bangor...well, he'd love to keep seeing her. Explore more dates and such. But he wasn't a forever partner.

The music ended. The couples around them all clung to each other for a moment. He was glad, because it meant that it wasn't obvious to anyone, but him, that he didn't let her go the moment the music stopped.

"Guess it's time to get back on the bus and then grab some beauty rest." Violet pulled back but put her hand in his as they followed the rest of the crowd out.

"I had fun tonight, Vi. A lot of it."

"Even if my college bestie threatened you?" She giggled as they stepped onto the party bus.

"Fiona didn't threaten me—technically." She'd never actually uttered the threat.

Sliding onto the bench seat, Violet pulled him down next to her. "I think we both know not uttering it is more threatening."

True.

CHAPTER EIGHT

VIOLET PULLED HER shoes off as soon as she and Beck stepped into their hotel room. She stretched her toes. "I know they aren't everyone's favorite footwear, but I'll take the comfy orthopedic shoes I wear with my scrubs over heels every single day."

Perfection.

That was the best descriptor for tonight. That was something she hadn't counted on when she ran into Thomas and his new wife by the elevator. Beck was the best date she could ask for. He might not have many moves on the dance floor, but he'd stood with her. Loosening up his hips and swishing to the music.

She'd seen the photographer snap a few photos of them. She'd have to ask Fiona to send one or two. Maybe this wasn't forever, but she wanted to document it. She felt alive around Beck.

Thomas had refused to set foot on the dance floor. He said he had two left feet. Maybe he did, but she thought the real issue was that he didn't want people watching him do something he wasn't very good at.

His wife had dutifully stood by him tonight. Violet hadn't paid them much attention. She hoped Dove was happy, but she was glad it wasn't her sitting out of the dances anymore.

"Sit. I'll rub your feet." Beck took off his jacket and tie.

He unbuttoned the top two buttons of his dress shirt, and she bit back the groan coming up her throat. No man had ever looked as good as Beck did.

"I can't ask you to do that." She kissed his cheek. Why couldn't she stop touching him, even though the nearly platonic touch wasn't close to what her body craved?

They'd shared that one kiss after karaoke. One glorious kiss. Since then…disappointment. No. Touching him and being touched by him were never disappointing. Violet just wanted more.

She grabbed her sweatpants and an old T-shirt. "I'm going grab a quick shower." Maybe if she was in the decidedly unsexy outfit, it would keep her thoughts in control.

Pulling her wet hair into a loose braid for sleeping, she took a deep breath. Beck was sweet, fun to hang out with and the perfect wedding date.

He was also gorgeous and she wanted another kiss. And so much more. If he kissed like a god, how would he make love? Slow, sensuously. Taking all night to…

Heat flooded her entire body. The sweats and oversize shirt were doing nothing to chill her own need.

Straightening her shoulders, she tried to put the desire into a mental box. He'd mentioned dating—and then the shift from hell and exhaustion had ruined that. They were having a good time at a wedding. That was all.

Stepping out of the bathroom, she nearly fell over the scene he made on the bed. The only one bed in the room. He'd said he'd use the pullout couch, but she'd told him there was no reason they couldn't behave as adults and share.

Now, though, she wondered if she could make it.

Beck was in a tight white undershirt and loose blue sweatpants. He was reading a book, his glasses just a little lower on the edge of his nose. He looked like an underwear model.

Looking over the spine, he grinned, then set the book down. "Come here." He held up some of the lotion she'd brought with her.

"What?" Her mouth went dry as her mind started to spin fantasies.

"Your feet." Beck pointed. "I know a shower can help, but those shoes looked vicious and you have to be in them tomorrow too. So come on."

He patted the bed and her knees buckled. "Beck—"

"You aren't asking, I'm offering. Let me take care of you."

Take care of you.

When was the last time any man had taken care of her? She racked her brain but not a single instance ran through her head. Sure, there'd been times when she'd asked Thomas for help, or asked one of her other boyfriends for something, but they'd never actually taken care of her.

In fact, Thomas had made certain she never felt comfortable asking. A red flag she hoped he'd corrected before marrying his new wife.

"Thank you." She scooted onto the bed and put her feet over his lap. Even through the two layers of sweats between them, she could feel the heat of his body. Or maybe it was just her imagination playing through something so delicious.

Beck put some of the lotion on her feet. "Oh, this smells nice." He gripped her right foot, his fingers lying over the top as his thumbs pressed the bottom of her foot an inch or so beneath her toes.

"Ohhh." The sigh flew out of her mouth as his thumbs circled the pressure points. She'd meant to say something about that being her daily moisturizing lotion. It had a pleasant scent, but it wasn't a strong perfume. However, all the words fell from her brain as he touched her.

"Lean back."

The command was soft, but she was incapable

of doing anything but following. "How did you get so good at this?"

Beck slid off the bed, pulling her feet with him so that they were at the edge of the bed, while he knelt on the floor.

"My mother. In her last few years, her feet hurt terribly from nerve pain, but she had dementia and couldn't remember any new people. She didn't remember me, either, or at least not that I was her son. But she knew that I was safe; so she let me rub her feet. It calmed her and made it a little easier for her to walk short distances."

She leaned up on her elbows looking over at him. "I bet she liked that."

He titled his head, but didn't look up from her feet, the pressure never stopping.

"She did. They had me late in life. The surprise baby. Dad had been gone for a year when she had to go into assisted living. I think of them often, and I bet they are having a blast together on the other side. Maybe even traveling to different parts of the universe."

That was such a nice thought. A tinge sad, but she could hear the happy memories even in his grief.

Violet hadn't had a close relationship with her parents. Her mother had filed the divorce papers the day after Violet moved out. Both parents seemed to blame her for how their lives had turned out. Or maybe she was just a reminder of the decades of life with a partner they'd hated.

If they'd asked, she'd have preferred two homes to the broken one she'd grown up in.

They fell into an oddly comforting silence.

"All right, my hands are aching. How are your feet?"

Oh. Violet sat up, stretched and wiggled her toes. "I feel great. I'm so sorry. I should have paid more attention to the time."

Beck waved his hand like he was brushing the apology away. "I'm fine." He grinned and headed into the bathroom.

She felt amazing. And she planned to return the favor.

When he came back out of the bathroom, he sat on the bed and she could smell the minty tooth-paste.

"Let me have your hand." She didn't wait for him to say anything.

Pulling his left hand into hers, she lifted his palm and ran her thumb down the middle. Fiona had taken a course in medical massage in college. Her friend had focused on hands and shoulders, since that was where most people kept most of the tension.

"Ohhh. I'm not the only one with a secret skill." Beck groaned and held up his other palm as soon as she touched it.

"Well, you don't have to be in heels all day, but it will be a long day for you, too."

Beck wrapped his fingers around hers. "Vi." His blue gaze captured hers.

The hotel room was a decent size, but in this moment, it felt like there was nowhere to go to escape his jeweled eyes.

Like I want to go anywhere.

"Beck." His name tasted so good on her tongue. Before she could think of anything else, she leaned forward. Her lips brushed his and the world exploded.

Vi was kissing him. Really kissing him. For no reason. There was no one to impress in this room. No ex, so no need to make a point. No questions to avoid.

No learning moment or silly bet.

Just Beck and Vi.

Heaven.

That was what this hotel room was. A slice of perfection. Their slice of perfection.

His hands cupped her face, willing her to come a little closer. She scooted toward him, her legs wrapping around his waist.

Heaven.

"Beck." She kissed him again. Her hands circled his back as she fit against him.

The cotton shirt he wore was fire against his skin. Dear God he ached to pull it off. Take her shirt off and spend the evening losing himself in her body.

And he would too. There were no illusions here. Vi was the most beautiful, kind, sweet, funny woman he'd ever met. He'd accept any exhaustion in order to spend the next several hours worshiping her body.

But tomorrow was her friend's wedding. She was bridesmaid and had responsibilities from the moment breakfast ended to the end of the reception.

"Vi." He cupped the back of her neck. "Vi."

"You already said my name." She grinned, then kissed him again. The feel of her smile against his lips was a huge turn on.

"You have a big day tomorrow." He pulled back, feeling every bit of the playful pout she gave him.

Moving her hips against him, he had no doubt she knew how turned on he was. "It is going to be very busy indeed. All the more reason to release some tension tonight."

"Mmm." He raised a brow. "Taking care of your tension is not an issue." Beck slid his fingers down her back.

She tipped her head and dropped her hand to the bulge in his lap. "You are tense too."

He gripped her hand, pulling it to his lips, where he kissed each finger while holding her chocolate gaze. "I am. But the first time I sleep with you, I plan to make it last as long as possible."

Violet looked at him, then looked over her shoulder at the hotel clock on the nightstand. Recognition crossed her gaze. It was already so late.

"Tomorrow?"

"Mmm-hmm." Tomorrow. He'd get to spend the entire day planning out exactly how he wanted to make her come. Not a bad way to spend the day. The expectation alone would have them both in perfect sync.

"But for now." He put his hands around her back, leaning her against the pillows.

"Is this the part where you put me to bed? Not sure I can sleep quite yet." She grinned and kissed him, her teeth nipping at his bottom lip.

"Why don't you let me help with that?" Beck trailed kisses down her neck. "Untie your sweatpants, Vi."

She took a deep breath and followed the command.

Beck slipped his hand down her pants, stroking her through her silky panties. He craved her nakedness, but if he stripped her, the minute control he was maintaining on his own need would crack.

The little cries echoing from her lips were going to drive him mad in his dreams tonight. He teased her mouth with his tongue before slipping his hand into her panties.

"Beck." She arched against him as he pressed

his thumb to her clit, circling the tiny bud, adjusting his pressure with each sigh he drew from her lips.

"Beck!"

The soft pant drew a moan from him. "Vi."

"I like you calling me Vi. No one else does." The words were broken with pants.

She was close, and he slipped a finger into her, his thumb never shifting its pressure. She broke as he stroked her core, his name on her lips as she crested the mountain.

Vi didn't break his gaze as he pulled his hand from her pants. Neither of them had discarded any clothes, but he'd never been more turned on.

Tomorrow.

"Think you can sleep tonight?" Beck slid onto the pillow beside her.

"Beck." His name was a sigh on her lips, the result of her orgasm and exhaustion. He pulled her into his arms.

"Good night, Vi." He kissed the top of her head, holding her tightly as her soft sighs disappeared as she drifted off to sleep.

Heaven.

Well rested did not even begin to describe her this morning. She'd slept like the dead, and awakened in Beck's arms. He'd snoozed beside her, but she was very aware of the erection pressing against her thigh.

Unfortunately there'd been no time for her to relieve his "tension." The bridal party and families were meeting for breakfast, then the bride and bridesmaids were headed to the suite Fiona had booked for the day for hair, makeup and bridal day fun.

"The buffet looks good." The words felt stilted after what they'd shared last night. What did one say in the morning after you'd had the best orgasm ever and never even dropped your drawers? Though his command to untie her pants had featured in several of her dreams she'd had last evening.

"It does. Are you hungry?" There was a hint of a sparkle in his eye.

She was ravenous. For food...and him.

Heat warmed her cheeks, and she had to look away from Beck's blue eyes. Seriously, if the flame went out on the heaters keeping the sausages warm, she was pretty sure her touch alone would reignite it.

They grabbed their food and headed to one of the open four-seat tables.

"Do you have plans while I'm spending the day getting all dolled up?" Violet asked the question just as Beck put a big bite of egg in his mouth.

"Sorry." She giggled.

"That was less than perfect timing." Beck grinned as he reached for his coffee. "I don't really have any plans. I'm going to ask the concierge what is around besides the Frost Museum of Science, since we are getting an up close and personal version of that for the wedding tonight."

"Text me any fun pictures." There wasn't time for her to have much of a tourist jaunt this time, but she hadn't lived and worked in this city in a decade so she wouldn't have been a helpful guide anyway.

"Of course."

"Violet." Thomas's tone broke through her morning joy and she didn't bother to smile as he and his wife set their food down at the two open chairs.

Surely the man didn't want to have breakfast with her and Beck. "Thomas, there are open seats—"

"These work fine." He pulled out a napkin and spread it across his lap. The people at the table next to them had turned their heads, and heat poured onto her cheeks. How many times had he made her feel uncomfortable before?

Countless.

And his poor wife. In the morning light, it was clear how much they looked alike. She didn't meet Violet's gaze as she stabbed a fork through the cut strawberry on her plate.

This was beyond awkward.

Beck caught her gaze and raised an eyebrow. If she wanted him to make a scene he would. But this was Fiona's wedding day. At least a handful of the people down here were wedding guests. If this became a hissy fit, and Thomas was not above that, then guests would gossip over it at the wedding. It was just human nature.

She was not going to be gossip—that was the entire reason Beck was here!

"I wanted to talk to you." Thomas cleared his throat, picked up his knife and fork but didn't cut his food.

Beck's right hand slid along her knee. At least she wasn't facing her ex and her look-a-like alone.

"We haven't seen each other or talked in years. I don't know what there is to discuss. We are just here to celebrate Fiona and Patrick." Violet laid her hand over Beck's, squeezing it once. With any luck Thomas would take the hint—for the first time in his life.

"I want the royalties for our book. All of them."

Direct had never been a problem for Thomas, but she hadn't even finished one cup of coffee. No workup to it. No beating around the bush.

"You aren't training dogs in Maine. This one told me that last night." Thomas pointed his still unused fork at Beck.

She hadn't trained dogs in Maine, hadn't thought of training them, until she'd met up with Beck at the Happy Feet Gym. But even if she wasn't training them, she'd written the book. Sure, his name was on it, but all he'd contributed was gripes.

"Vi does train. I just didn't want to discuss it with you." Beck let out an overdramatic sigh. "She is my girlfriend, man. You left her at the altar. You don't get to know her present. Why can't you see that?"

Thomas blinked at Beck's rebuke.

Violet leaned over and kissed Beck's cheek. She laid a hand on the other side of his face. "Thank you."

"So you are training?"

"She is working with our intermediate team. The first session she had with us was life-changing."

"Beck." That was a bit of an overstatement. The one training session they'd had was good. And there'd been immediate improvements, but life-changing was not even close to a description she'd use.

"No. You are amazing. In fact with your training, I bet we place this year at regionals. A first for the gym." Beck's gaze was fully focused on her.

She could hear Thomas's huff, and she knew he could, too. But Beck never broke her gaze.

"Thank you."

"A small gym in Maine does not make you a full-time trainer. I could take you to court over the royalties. Make it clear to them that I'm the real brains behind the book and that I only let you get your name on it because we were, ahem, involved at the time." That was an empty threat.

They'd signed a contract with the publishing house who'd insisted they have separate contracts since they weren't legally married. A small grace that she hadn't been grateful for at the time. She'd had a lawyer look at it after Thomas left, just in case he pulled this kind of stunt.

It had taken longer than she'd expected, but there was no way for him to sue for such a thing. And if he did, he'd lose and have to pay her court fees. But...

"You never gave my grandmother's tablecloth back. What on earth makes you think I'd be willing to do a single thing for you." She crossed her arms. Nana had cross-stitched the little gingerbread family and Christmas trees and given it to Violet as an engagement gift. The fact that Thomas had taken it and refused to even acknowledge he had it when she'd texted him repeatedly was low enough. The idea that he and his family were using it, a gift for her, from her nana, a woman who hadn't lived to see him leave her at the altar.

A small blessing, for her nana would have hunted him down.

"I don't have the tablecloth."

"You do." She grabbed her phone, opened the pictures and spun it toward him. "I snapped that pic of your table when Fiona reposted a picture of the tablecloth that your mother took last Christmas."

She saw Dove's eye widen, but Thomas's wife didn't add anything to the conversation. That was fine. This wasn't her fight.

Thomas looked at the photo, let out a sigh, then lifted the coffee cup to his lips. He took a long sip, his eyes never leaving her face. Once that stare might have made her stand down. Now all it did was make her straighten her back and raise her chin.

"That isn't your tablecloth. And we are discussing the book." A book that at this point wasn't bringing in many royalties. Maybe it was time for another—without Thomas's name on it.

The thought punched through her brain. Another…

There was so much she'd left out of the first book. Trainer's Guide Version Two had been her pretend nickname for an idea she'd let die when Thomas walked out of her life. Another thing she'd let him steal.

"I guess this conversation is over. See you in Boston for the regionals—with your team." Thomas pushed back from the table.

"Just so you know." Beck leaned forward, and she saw Thomas startle just a little. "As a show of goodwill you should give that tablecloth back. It would be a shame if news like that went viral in social media posts. I'm sure everyone who fre-

quents your gym and still has great memories of
Violet would be shocked to learn you took that."

"Who says they have great memories?"

Vi tilted her head, imagining her fingers wrapping around his stupid little neck.

"Of course they have great memories of Vi. She
is the best." Beck put an arm around her shoulders, and all the murderous thoughts evaporated
as he planted his lips on hers.

Beck was staking a claim. Letting Thomas
know that he was no longer important in her life.
Usually Violet hated that kind of male protection,
but with Beck, part of her wished it was real.

CHAPTER NINE

"WHERE DID YOU learn to dance?" Beck wasn't ashamed to admit that there was no way to keep up with Vi on the dance floor. Luckily, she didn't seem bothered by his awkward movements.

And she had an innate ability to dodge his feet if they strayed too close to her toes.

Vi let out a giggle as she twirled through his arms with the fast beat. "I signed up for class by mistake."

The song ended and the DJ started a ballad. Finally. Pulling Violet into his arms was a lovely, but it also let him catch his breath. They'd been on the dance floor since the bride and groom opened it with their first dance. And he suspected they'd close it down.

Which was fine with him.

"How does one sign up for a dance class by mistake?" He'd taken dozens of classes over time. More extreme ones after his parents passed. Sky-diving certifications, deep-sea diving, hang gliding...anything that sparked his interest and got his blood pumping. But never by mistake.

Violet laid her head against his shoulder. There were others on the dance floor, but they evaporated as he kissed her and spun her slowly around the floor.

"I filled out paperwork at the little hobby shop in my hometown. They had all sorts of things and I spent most of my childhood summers there. I meant to sign up for the stained-glass crafting course, but I transposed the numbers and ended up in beginning jazz. I *was not* dressed correctly for that first class let me tell you."

"I bet." Beck pulled her even closer, letting his finger run down her back. The navy bridesmaid dress had a classic, modest, scoop neck. But the back had nearly sent him to his knees when he watched her walk down the aisle.

The deep vee opened nearly to the top of her perfect ass. There was no way she was wearing more than pasties over her taut breasts. A single pearl drop necklace hung down the middle of her back. It was formal and sexy as hell. "Never did learn how to craft stained glass. I did take every dance class I could fit in my schedule. In fact, I took so many in college I actually earned a double major in biology and dance."

"Have you taken any classes at Spotlight Studios?" He didn't know much about dance classes, but he'd been to more than one recital. A few years ago his friend Marcus's little boy had signed up for tap. He had almost backed out of the recital because he'd been made fun of in school. Marcus had called on all his friends to sit in the front row and cheer him on.

Last year his son had started modern dance, and the whole cheering section was right in place to cheer him on. It was fun. When it was time for the spring recital, he'd have to make sure to invite Violet. She'd love it.

His feet stumbled, and Vi grabbed his shoulders.

"Careful there!" She kissed his cheek.

"Sorry." It was weird to be glad that he'd nearly smashed her toes several times tonight. But it meant that Violet wouldn't think this was anything more than a rhythm misstep rather than his heart breaking a little.

He didn't know what this fling would look like, but he doubted it included bringing Vi to a yearly event—even one he knew she'd love. It hurt to think that she wouldn't be next to him.

That was a problem for future Beck. The list of things his future self would have to deal with was adding up, but he wasn't going to think of them.

Right now he was focusing on the woman in front of him. On the woman coming alive before him.

"Since I nearly mashed your toes, you didn't

answer. Have you taken any dance classes since you moved to Bangor?"

She stiffened in his arms and the song changed before she answered. She bolted from his arms without a word. Not that he really needed a verbal answer.

The Violet he'd known for the past few years and the woman who'd been dancing in his arms were two different creatures. Both were magnificent. But he couldn't help but feel like the Violet currently holding the bride's hips as they started a conga line was the real version.

Would she stay this person when they returned to Bangor? Or would she put this form of herself back into hibernation? As the conga line stretched around the room, he joined in, enjoying the smile Vi passed back as the giant snake of wedding guests enjoyed the silly dance.

"Now that that has ended..." the DJ said as Violet found her way back to Beck.

"I could use a glass of water." She wrapped an arm around his waist.

"I'm parched." Beck brushed her lips with his as they turned to head off the dance floor.

They hadn't taken two steps when the DJ continued. "Time for all the unmarried ladies to make their way to the dance floor. It's bouquet toss time, and Fiona has a twist for it."

"Of course she does." Violet giggled as Fiona

moved onto the dance floor carrying her bouquet with at least a dozen ribbons attached to it.

"Come on, single ladies! I know who all of you are, and I have a ribbon for each of you *with* your name on it! You are not getting out of my game!"

Violet shook her head as Fiona made direct eye contact with her.

"I think that last part was a dig at you." Beck tapped her hip with his and kissed the top of her head. "Go. I'll have refreshments ready as soon as you step off the floor."

"If she wasn't the bride…" Violet kissed him, then made her way to the group, grabbing the lone ribbon on the floor.

Fiona told the women they were doing a bridal maypole and when she cut their ribbon they were out. Then she pulled a sleep mask over her eyes, raised the bouquet above her head and the music started.

Fiona seemed to take her time using the scissors, though maybe it was harder to cut ribbon blindfolded than she'd counted on.

Thomas sidled up to Beck, who grimaced. What had Violet ever seen in this awful man?

"You know this is what she wants, right? Better hope Violet doesn't get that bouquet if you aren't ready to pop the question."

Beck did not bother to address that ridiculous statement.

Unfortunately his silence didn't seem to be

a deterrent for Thomas. "For as long as I knew Violet, she talked of getting married. Having a happy life with a partner. Nights in and all that jazz." Thomas crossed his arms as he stood next to Beck, his gaze focused on the single ladies in the center.

One lady in particular.

"Do you have a point? Or are you just not over her? I get it. She is remarkable. I'd hate losing that." His mouth suddenly dried as he realized he'd lose it too.

They were faking that they'd been together six months for the wedding—not that anyone had asked more than a handful of questions about how they met before moving onto other topics.

Thomas bristled and let out a low grunt. "I did not lose her. I was the one who ended things. Because I didn't want to be tied down."

Beck did not bother to argue that he was married now. To a woman who had to be questioning why her husband had an ex-fiancée who could be mistaken for her.

"Whoever is lucky enough to spend their life with Vi will never describe it as tied down." Jealousy flashed across his brain. Whoever that faceless person was would be forever lucky to have her by their side.

Getting to wake up next to her. Joke with her. Dance with her. That life was not going to be his. He wasn't ready to be married.

And Vi hadn't mentioned marriage.

Why would she?

Fiona cut the last string—Vi's string. For a moment he saw her face falter. She'd wanted the bouquet.

The moment was over before anyone else probably even noticed. She rolled up her ribbon and danced over to the woman now holding a miniature of Fiona's bouquet. She was laughing, all smiles. No hint of jealousy.

No doubt she was happy for her friend. But Thomas was right. Vi wanted marriage. She wanted to be the one tossing the bouquet or cutting the ribbon or whatever.

That wasn't a life he was ready for. Wasn't a life he was even sure he wanted.

We are having a fling. I shouldn't care that she wants more at some point in the future. With someone else.

Vi knew where they stood. This was fun. So why the hell did watching her dance with her ribbon above her head as the winner passed the bouquet around make him feel so empty?

Violet was exhausted. Fiona and Patrick's day had been perfect. That was what mattered. Right now she wanted exactly three things:

1. Kick off her high heels.
2. A shower.
3. Beck.

Pretty much in that order. Though she wouldn't mind joining number two and three together. As they got to the hotel door, she didn't bother to wait to start on number one, yanking the shoes off before Beck swung the door open.

"How are your feet?" Beck looked down at the toes that had been pinched most of the day and were certainly less than pretty at the moment.

Not where she wanted his focus.

"Sore." There was no point in fibbing. "But they will be fine. I'm going to grab a shower." She hesitated, then just decided to go for it. "Want to join me?"

Beck dropped his tux coat on the chair and pulled at the black tie he'd loosened in the elevator. "There isn't a lot of room in that shower." His voice was low. Husky.

Her body heated as she stepped toward him.

"I promise not to steal all the hot water, if that is what you are concerned about."

The grin spread across his face, and the dimples she was so fond of appeared. "I'm starting the water." She turned and had to breathe deeply so that she didn't run to the bathroom.

Not that she wanted to flee. No. What she wanted was to take that sexy man, push him to the bed and have her way with him. Something she very much planned to accomplish after the day's makeup, hairspray and sweat were wiped from her body.

She started the water and felt his hands skim her back.

"I don't know if you picked this dress or if Fiona chose it, but Vi—it's the sexiest thing I've ever seen." His hands danced across the top of her ass, just below the cut of the dress.

"Fiona let us choose. They just all had to be navy. I will admit, since I ordered it online with just my measurements at the shop, I was more than a little stunned at how low the back cut was."

Fiona had screamed when she saw it during the try on when it was delivered to Violet's local dress shop from the Miami shop she'd ordered it from. If Fiona had been there in person instead of on a video call, she might have blown Violet's eardrums out. Fiona had clapped as she did a happy dance, then immediately suggested a statement back necklace. If there was one thing you could count on with Fiona as your friend, it was that she was going to root for you no matter what.

"This dress is going to feature in so many of my dreams." Beck's lips pressed against her shoulder as his hand traveled up her back then lowered again.

Violet turned and his hands cupped her butt, pulling her close.

"I need to pull the pins out of my hair so I can wash the hairspray out." She kissed his cheek and stepped to the mirror. The shower wasn't huge, but the bathroom was a very nice size overall.

Beck's hands strayed from her ass and he pulled
one hairpin, then another and another from her
dark locks. His fingers gently rubbing her scalp
as his mouth trailed kisses down her neck. Was
there nothing this man wasn't good at?

Commitment.

Her brain supplied the answer without prompt-
ing, but Violet forced it away. She wasn't looking
for commitment. She was looking for a fun time
with a sexy man who wanted her. And Beck fit
all of those criteria.

"I think I got all of them." Beck breathed the
words against her ear as his hand cupped the back
of her neck.

"Thank you." The words were thick. Every part
of her body was alive, and he'd barely touched her.

"Take your dress off, Vi."

The command rocketed through her system.
All she could do was obey. All she wanted to do
was obey.

The straps of her dress slid down her arms,
her body operating on pure desire as she stared
at him. Steam swirled around them.

He unbuttoned his shirt and tossed it to the
floor.

Her hands dragged along his abs, and she let
out a soft sigh. Of course he looked even better
shirtless.

Beck hooked a finger into the navy panties
she'd bought for the day. The lacy undergarment

was at her feet in seconds and the only thing standing between her and nakedness was the pasties she'd worn.

"I knew you were only in pasties." His thumb circled the silicone patch.

"Can't exactly wear a bra with that dress." Violet nipped his lip as she reached for the button of his tux pants. She was basically naked, and she wanted him wearing nothing at all too.

His pants lowered to the floor and she felt him step out of them, but his mouth never left hers. "Come on. Into the shower." He turned her, his hand giving her ass the slightest push.

"The pasties."

"Will come off easier in the water." His lips trailed along her shoulder blade. "I plan to spend the entire night worshiping your body. I don't want anything sore."

His touch was electric, his kisses sublime. But it was the care he was showing on such a simple thing. The pasties had been on for more than eight hours and stayed on through the wedding and an evening of dancing.

She stepped into the shower. The hot water hit her back and she ached to stay under it, but she moved to let Beck stand in the water. The few times she'd showered with Thomas he'd insisted on standing in the water.

Beck gently grabbed her hips and pulled her into the water.

"You'll get cold." Her words were soft as his fingers stroked up her stomach then lower but never to where she ached for him most.

"*I* will be fine. You are the one who had a long day. I got to roam Miami, checking out anything I fancied, then spend the night dancing with the most interesting woman in the whole city." Beck reached for the soap, worked a lather up in his hands then started working his way along her body.

"Mmm." Violet leaned her head back. The heat of the shower and his touch melted together in a delicious manner there were no descriptors for.

His hands circled her breasts, soap and warm water making quick work of the pasties. Then his thumbs were circling her nipples.

"Beck…"

"Turn around, Vi."

She was putty in his hands. She turned on command, very aware of the thick rod against her butt. Violet wiggled her ass against it, enjoying the hiss of breath as he tried to stay focused on her.

He poured a little shampoo into his hands, then started working it through her hair. "Mmm."

"I like it when I steal all the words from you." Beck kissed the soft skin behind her ears as he washed her hair.

She thrust her back against his length and he made the same little hiss as he rushed the air out. "And *I* enjoy making you do that."

He turned her to allow the water to start rinsing the shampoo from her locks. When it was gone, she grabbed the conditioner, finished up her hair routine, then pulled him into the water.

Last night he'd touched her. Brought her to completion with no demand for his own need. Tonight…tonight she was going to touch him. She soaped up her hands, then let herself explore Beck with the same enthusiasm he'd done to her.

As she wrapped her hands around his length, he let out a groan. "Vi."

The nickname on his lips as she stroked him was such a turn on.

His hand slipped between her legs, finally gliding over the sensitive spot she craved. It vanished so fast as he turned the water off.

"If we stand in here in any longer, I'm going to lose myself, Vi." He grabbed a towel from the rack and wrapped her in it, before grabbing another and drying himself faster than she thought possible.

I guess anything is possible when you're motivated.

She stepped out of the shower. Steam filled the whole room. Beck followed her, grabbing a spare towel to pull the excess moisture from her hair.

"Beck." The care was lovely, and excruciating.

"I want you, Vi. I want you more than I've ever wanted anyone or anything." Beck's lips lingered on hers as he dropped the towel to the floor, then reached for the one wrapped around her body.

He pulled it away, reached for the bathroom door, then gathered her into his arms.

There was nothing Beck wanted more than to bury himself in Violet and lose himself in the sensation. But he'd sworn that during their first time together he was going to worship her. And there was so much of her left to adore.

Carrying her to the bed, he laid her gently on the edge, then he spread her legs and licked her core. He'd longed to do this last night.

Strip her. Taste her. Lose himself in the perfection of Vi.

"Beck."

His name on her lovely lips made him harder—something that shouldn't have been possible.

Slipping his hands under her butt, he pulled her even closer, drinking her in. Her legs wrapped around his head, urging him more as her fingers wrapped in his hair. She was panting, her hips bucking as his tongue darted around her clit.

"Beck!" She moaned his name, but this time as he felt her crest over the edge. He pulled one hand from under her and grabbed the condom he'd laid out on top of the nightstand this morning.

He didn't stop kissing her as he pulled the sheath from its wrapping and slid it down his length.

"Beck. Seriously. I need you. Now. Now."

He grinned against her thigh as trailed a line of kisses there. "I like it when you demand that."

Beck slipped between her legs, pushing himself in just a little and sucking in a deep breath.

"No teasing. Please, please." Violet wrapped her legs around his hips, pulling him deeper.

His fingers moved through her hair as his lips caught hers. "Not teasing. Just trying to keep from losing myself so completely in a second."

Violet claimed his mouth as he filled her.

Once joined, their bodies moved as one, their breathing seeming to synchronize as she climaxed again. Finally he let himself experience the same release.

CHAPTER TEN

"NICE WORK!" Violet clapped as Tim and Pickle did a perfect 270-degree transition and raced onto the A-frame then across the finish line.

Beck and Toaster were at the starting line; Beck celebrating, Toaster looking at the course, ready for her turn. That dog lived for agility.

Since returning from Miami last week, she and Bear had spent a few days at Beck's after shift. The two of them had agreed when the fling started that it went on for as long as they both wanted it. And that no one was getting down on one knee.

It was easy with Beck. There were no expectations—just fun. It was nice. But there was a heaviness that she couldn't always force away.

This was the life she'd planned. Working as a vet, running an agility team and coming home to a partner who made her feel like she was the best catch in the world. For years she'd put that life away. Refused to acknowledge the dream she'd held for so long. Now she had part of it.

As she watched Beck start Toaster off on the course, she swallowed the small lump in the back of her throat. They were having fun. He wasn't a forever partner, but that was all right, for now.

"Good job, Toaster." Beck laughed as the dog jumped into his arms at the end of the course.

"It was a good run," Violet said as she joined them.

"But?" Beck raised an eyebrow.

"But, Toaster is still not comfortable with the blind approaches." The dog was hesitating on obstacles that were not clear from the dismount from the last obstacle. It was a common issue.

Dogs wanted to see their whole path. They wanted to know what was coming. It was a natural response that could cost points in a competition.

A competition she wanted this team to place in. Thomas was going to be there, and he was going to judge how they did. Kicking his ass would be such a great way to put the final nail in the coffin of her past.

She should have told him to stick it when he asked for the royalties of the book. Having that much audacity was a skill—one that she hated to admit had gotten him access to places he really had no business being.

A mediocre man riding the coattails of others did not deserve anything. Unfortunately she knew he was petty enough to refuse to return the tablecloth…or even destroy it. Having it was his cruel reminder to her that he'd taken something she couldn't replace.

"Toaster has always struggled with blind approaches." Beck passed his dog a training treat, rewarding her for the good run. And it had been a good run—just not great.

"Well, we have a couple more weeks before regionals in Boston. So we will focus on everyone's main issues. Toaster doesn't like blind obstacles, Posy is not a fan of the collapsed tunnel, Tuna had multiple contact faults tonight where she didn't touch the obstacle the right way and Pickle barely got over the bar."

"Barely." Tim smiled. "But she cleared it and that means no dropped bar fault."

"Her back legs were millimeters from it, Tim. If she is nervous at competition, which is always possible, those millimeters will be an easy slip for her." She'd told the team about her ex. About how she'd love for the Happy Feet Gym to crush the fancy gym she'd used to work at. They'd all rally around to do their best to place.

Which she was grateful for. But it meant they were going to have to work harder than anyone but Nancy had worked at Happy Feet. Tonight was their first full workout. The first real test.

"Okay, but I mean, she cleared it. I get what you are saying but," he said, shrugging, "I don't get why we are focusing on a dropped bar that didn't drop."

She looked at the group and their dogs. "I know this is hard." Maybe this was too much all at once. It was a lot to ask a team that usually used the trip as a fun excuse to get out of town for the weekend. But they were already so close. With just a bit of work they could clear the hurdles—literally and figuratively.

"Things that are worthwhile generally are." Beck nodded to her.

She gave him a quick smile. On the few occasions that Thomas had been on the gym floor with her, he'd vanished when even the smallest bit of conflict had arisen.

"They are." Violet took a deep breath. "If you have changed your minds and do not wish to aim for medals, that's fine. But we make that decision tonight. As a group. One person wants out, then we go to Boston for fun only. No pressure."

"What about your ex?" Grace covered her heart with her hand. "I mean come on. That guy sounds like he needs to be taken down at least one peg."

Grace had an ex-husband who was a real piece of work according to Beck. She was living a little vicariously through Vi's desire to stick it to Thomas. It was sweet, but this was a team effort.

"I appreciate the support. But this is your team. I am an interloper and asking a lot."

"You are our coach." Lisa crossed her arms.

"*Not* an interloper. Assuming you want to be our coach. I mean I know you are just getting back into agility and you have the vet clinic and Beck... dear God someone else say something so I can stop blathering."

Beck reached down and gave Toaster a rub behind her floppy ears. "You know I am in."

"Tim." Grace turned her focus on him and the others followed.

"Nope. Nope, we aren't ganging up on Tim." Violet stepped forward. "He gets to make his own decision."

"I choose the team and trying to medal. I'm sorry about the question."

"Don't apologize for questions." Violet had always had an open forum with her clients. She knew agility. Knew dogs. Knew competitions.

She knew coaches who felt that because they knew those things, it wasn't a client's position to question the coach. She felt no need to gatekeep the information.

"You asked why millimeters matter. The truth is that they may not, but if Pickle is tired before running the course from excitement, or nerves, or something she can't tell us about because she is a dog and we do not speak the same language then it might matter." Violet made a cute face at the dog as Pickle tilted her head as though she was absorbing everything from this very important conversation.

"If she is used to being just millimeters above the bar, then there is no room for error." Tim nodded. "Makes sense."

"It does." She put her hand out, palm down. The others followed suit, laying one hand on top of the other. "On three we yell team."

"One," Violet said as she looked to Grace.

"Two." Grace nodded at Beck.

"Three!" he roared.

"Team!" The cheer went up and the dogs all turned and looked at their humans like they'd lost their minds. But none of them barked or got excited.

That was good. Because the competition would be wild even though the dogs in attendance would be well behaved. Spectator noise. Scents galore. Excitement. It was a recipe for doggies to lose control.

"Nice work tonight. See everyone in two days." She waved to the group as Tim, Lisa and Grace gathered their pups and headed off.

"You are amazing. Do you know that?" Beck wrapped his arms around her. "You handled Tim with such skill."

"I was just answering his questions, Beck. Nothing special." She kissed his cheek, enjoying the feel of his arms wrapped around her.

He squeezed her and stepped back. "Why don't we grab Bear and let them play in the course for a little while. See if we can get Toaster a little more comfortable with blind approaches and get a little exercise for Bear."

"Hey." Violet playfully punched his shoulder. "Bear ran around a few times, and he went for a walk today. That is a lot of work for him."

"Uh-huh." Beck shook his head as he walked back out onto the course.

She went over to where Bear was sleeping. It wouldn't hurt for him to run a few more laps. The pittie would never be an agility competition dog, but he was a good boy.

"Come on, honey, let's go get a little exercise."

"Sorry we are just having a slow night." Beck slid onto the couch where Vi was already starting to pull up the streaming services.

"No need to apologize." She crossed her legs, putting the bowl of popcorn she'd popped in the center.

Tonight was supposed to be a fun date. He'd had the best plan. But at the last minute the surprise had to be rescheduled. It was perfect too. So much better than movies on the couch. A mini adventure right in town.

"I swear I had an idea." He'd talked it up too. Made such a big deal out of it. And now she was eating popcorn on his couch looking through horror flick choices.

Violet tilted her head as she met his gaze. "Beck, I wanted to hang out tonight. I was excited for the surprise, and I will be excited when it happens. But that does not mean that a night rummaging through the solid campy horror flicks you have available on your streaming services is not just as exciting. I like hanging out at home and relaxing just us."

Hanging out at home—his parents' favorite thing. It was nice. Better than nice. He could almost see why his parents gave up their adventures. *Almost.*

"Horror movies. I would have thought you were into rom-coms." She loved the idea of love—that was clear in the instant Fiona cut Vi's ribbon.

The woman who'd showed up in Miami for the wedding had come home to Maine. Vi didn't just go to work, go home and repeat the process. That was good, but he kept wondering when she might decide to end this fling and find the man who'd get down on one knee. The one who'd let her toss the bouquet and dance with her in an elegant white gown.

He hated that future man.

"I like rom-coms too. But there is something about silly horror flicks. The campy ones that are working too hard and have low budgets so obvious it's funny. Or the ones that follow the exact script of the one survivor—always a teen girl who is very into her virginity."

Beck didn't have much knowledge on the genre.

"I don't know that I have ever watched a horror flick."

Popcorn teetered on the edge of the bowl but somehow managed not to spill over as Violet turned toward him. "How! How, as a teen boy, did you not watch any of the *Friday the 13th* movies, or *Zombieland* or *Freddy vs Jason* or *Predator* or—"

"Whoa!" Beck held up his hands as well-known but, at least for him, unwatched franchises rattled out of Vi's mouth. "I know those movies but, if you keep listing flicks, I'm going to lose track fast."

Vi scooted a little closer to him on the couch. "Sorry, but I thought it was a staple of teen male experience to watch gory movies. Or at least to take girls to horror movies in the hopes that they would lean super close to you and snuggle during the whole movie."

He'd had some male friends who'd certainly used that dating route but not him. "My parents didn't think they were appropriate."

"I can see that. Nightmares and all."

"That is a reason most would use, but my mom thought that they leaned into stereotypes and focused too much on using sex as a weapon for murder. She is credited on one of dad's anthropology papers about how the roles ancient societies placed on purity can be seen in modern movie franchises."

"Wow." Vi's eyes were huge as she turned to look at the list of movies pulled up on the screen. "I bet that was an interesting paper."

"It was well received by my father's colleagues." He remembered them poring over papers, talking excitedly with each other. The papers seemed to be all over the house that year rather than confined to their study as they usually were.

"I still have it on the shelf in their study. That room is mostly the same as it was." It was their happy place. And he'd loved to admit that was the reason he couldn't change it. That would be the selfless reason. A son still tied to his lost parents.

But the truth was that it was his reminder room. His dad's desk, with the image of their wedding day and a garden tea party. His father's favorite pictures. The ones showing the "boring" life he was so proud of. Beck used it as a reminder not to get stuck under papers, under matrimony—at least not for a while.

None of that was happy date night stuff, though. And on a night where they were already doing something less than thrilling, he wasn't going to think about the static life his parents had lived here. "Did a boy take you to a horror movie and wrap his arms around you when you got scared? Is that why you like them so much?"

Vi laughed, but it held very little humor. "No. I started watching them long before I was allowed to date. My mom hated them. I mean like refused to be in the house when they were on. So whenever she and Dad were having a blowout, he'd pop one on in the living room, sit on the couch and wait for her to leave."

Beck wasn't sure what to say. There were thousands of ways to get into the genre, and he'd have guessed all of them before that. "So you and your dad watched the movies together?" It seemed like a weird way to bond with a parent.

"Oh no. Dad didn't watch them. He just started them so she would leave." Vi let out a sigh. "Neither were good communicators. But hey, at least I know pretty much every horror flick available in the last thirty years."

"Yeah. That is a bonus." Beck wasn't sure what to say to that. He could count on one hand the number of times he'd seen his parents fight. Oh sure, they disagreed, decently often even, but they'd talked and worked it out.

Fights, the ones that resulted in a few days of hurt feelings, were so far removed from his youthful experience.

"So let's see, if you have never seen a horror movie, what do we start with? *Friday the 13th* is very well-known, but given the original release date of the first flick, it hasn't aged well. *Chucky* movies are another option."

"What is your favorite? That seems like the perfect place to start." He knew nothing more than the general themes of each. He remembered a few of his friends talking about the *Saw* franchise when it came out. Mostly because of the murderer's creepy mask.

"I am partial to zombie flicks. So we will grab one of those…after." She grabbed the popcorn bowl, stood and walked over to put it on the mantel. "I want to believe in our little angels." She looked over to the beds where Toaster and Bear were currently resting—both sets of eyes focused on the popcorn bowl. "But I think leaving a bowl of popcorn out is a little too much temptation."

"Where are we going?" Beck stood.

"The study. I need to read that paper." She clapped. "I mean I'll never get to meet your parents. This seems like a fun get-to-know-you thing, plus anthropology and horror movies. I mean who wouldn't want to read that!"

Me.

He loved his parents. Missed them inordinately but their papers, the study, it was a reminder of all that they'd given up.

His mother had planned to get a PhD in women's studies—yes, she'd had a successful career as a civil engineer—but she'd never gone back to school. Something she'd talked about a lot in her dementia haze the last year. Hell, he'd even found her "filling out the paperwork" once on random sheets of paper in the long-term care facility.

His dad had gone on at least four trips a year before meeting his mother. He'd been fascinated by the motifs from the ancient world still driving modern ways. Threads of life and time he'd called it. Once he married his mother, the trips had gone from four, to one to none, so fast.

Still, it wouldn't take long to get the report and then see what Vi loved about zombie movies. And if she was happy, then so was he.

"Oh my gosh." Vi stepped into the study and he followed her.

The room still had the soft scent of his father's cologne. It wafted with the smell of paper and time. If Beck closed his eyes, he could see his father sitting in the chair, pointing out something to his mother, hugging her as she leaned into him.

They were like one. The years she'd spent on this side of the mortal coil without him had been the hardest. The dementia had stolen her memories of his death, but not the memory of their love. She looked for him until the day she joined him.

"Is this them?" She picked up the image from the desk. "I mean of course it is. You look just like your dad."

"I call that the boring picture." He grinned as he stepped toward her.

"Boring?" She ran a finger over the edge of the frame. "This isn't boring."

"It's a garden party, Vi." He looked at the image. His mom was holding a drink in her left hand, his father's hand in her right. He was looking at her as though there were no other partygoers while she talked to guests the camera captured in shadows on the ground only.

She looked at the photo one more time. "I guess we have different definitions of boring." She kissed his cheek and set the photo back down.

Beck swallowed the pain that truth sent through him. They had very different definitions of boring. Maybe one day settling down, giving up opportunities for traveling and excitement would seem better.

Hell, part of his brain had started whispering the second they'd turned the fake dating into an actual fling that this could be more. He'd fully accepted that this fling's timeline was in Vi's court. He'd stay as long as she wanted...but when she was ready to start the life she clearly still wanted, he'd step aside.

"Did your dad publish all these?" She looked at the bookcase, filled with Dr. Forester's name.

"Yes. Though most of them have his students listed as the primary author. After Dad made tenure, he used his name and support to help junior researchers get published but refused to take credit as the lead author." Beck ran his fingers over the books. It was one of his father's crowning achievements.

He'd often wondered if he'd seen his students as surrogate children. Probably.

"They sound lovely."

"They were." Beck looked around the room, his eyes falling on Vi. They'd have liked her.

No.

They'd have loved her. His father would have started talking about how he loved his "boring" life. His mother would have offered her engagement ring. A family heirloom passed on by her grandmother. One he still had upstairs, not that he planned to give it to anyone.

They'd have seen the spark that Vi brought to everything.

"Here is the paper." He grabbed it, eager to leave this room. The memories here were sweet, a little sad, but they were dangerously close to making him want the boring life. Movies, a standard spaghetti night—Thursdays, matching holiday pjs. A settled life.

There was nothing wrong with that. It just wasn't what he planned…at least not yet.

"Wonderful. I'll get it back to you as soon as I'm through." Vi grabbed his hand. "Now…the zombies."

She held up her free hand, opening and closing her mouth and crossing her eyes.

He chuckled at the ridiculous scene. "Is that what zombies act like?"

Violet shook her head, a playful frown pulling at her perfect lips. "The fact that you even have to ask that." She kissed his cheek. "Let the horror movie education begin!"

CHAPTER ELEVEN

"So I was thinking the next time we have a down night, maybe we try *28 Days Later*. It's nearly thirty years old, but the zombies are fast and don't live forever." Beck winked before he headed into the on-call suite where a patient with a dog who they thought might have eaten a sock was waiting for an X-ray.

"Zombie movies. Not my thing." Lacey shook her head as she filled up her coffee mug and headed back out to the reception desk.

Violet liked zombie movies, and she was enjoying the fact that Beck apparently *really* liked zombie movies. It should be an exciting moment. Something for them to bond over.

So why did he keep insinuating that movie nights were down nights or boring? He'd apologized so many times for the movie night they'd had at his place three days ago. She wasn't sure what exciting event he'd had planned, but she knew it wasn't watching movies with a lap full of popcorn.

And then there'd been the picture of his parents. "The boring one" as he termed it. What she'd seen was happiness, love, life all wrapped into one photo. She knew why it held the place of honor on his father's desk.

Yes, the pictures of him in the Andes Mountains were exquisite and the image of his mother backpacking through Italy was gorgeous, but they didn't have the same life to them. The garden party perfectly captured two people, who according to Beck, had loved each other until the day they died.

If the universe was fair, they'd found each other on the other side and continued their journey together.

That was a kind of love her parents had never had. A kind of love she'd yearned for her whole life. That yearning had led her to nearly walk down the aisle to the wrong man. And then she'd spent ten years worrying it simply didn't exist.

But it did. People found it. People clung to it. How could Beck think that was boring?

It didn't matter. This was a fling. They were having fun.

Why do I have to keep reminding myself of that?

"Vi, the X-ray shows something in Roxy's large intestine." Beck walked to the screen in the back of the clinic, pushed a few things on the tablet and pulled up the image.

The sock was clear on the screen. Along with at least two others.

Crossing her arms, she blew out a breath. She'd hoped to prescribe some laxatives to the golden doodle if the X-ray showed a blockage. It wasn't uncommon for dogs to eat things they shouldn't— and it was a breed trait in goldendoodles.

Passing one sock might be possible, though there was never a guarantee. Passing three or more, would not be happening.

"How are the rest of her stats?" Maybe they could put off surgery until it was a standard business operating time. The procedure would still be expensive, but it would cut at least a thousand dollars off the bill.

"Not great. She's restless, and I had to muzzle her to do the exam. Roxy is dehydrated and no longer eating." Beck looked at his watch.

He was thinking the same thing she was. Roxy's owner, Marcy, loved her animal but for at least three socks, two hours on anesthesia and the emergency surcharge, it was going to be nearly five thousand dollars. Not a small price tag for anyone but a giant one for Marcy.

The woman had taken on the doodle after her sister had tired of the dog. A sweet and honorable decision. But, while all dogs were work, doodles required grooming, exercise to wear out their exuberant personalities and constant vigilance to keep them from doing things like attempting to digest socks.

Marcy did her best but tonight was going to be rough.

"All right. Let's go discuss options." She took one more look at the scan, then followed Beck to check on Roxy.

The dog was muzzled and lying against Marcy. Even without the X-ray the bulge in the lower belly was clear.

"I kept yelling at Trevor to pick up his damn socks. I told the bastard to pack his things while I'm here. It's one thing to ignore all the household chores while focusing on making your hacky sack YouTube videos, refuse to do a damn thing to help out with bills but to forget socks so Roxy gets sick. There is only so much I can take." Marcy buried her head in Roxy's ears, tears running down her face.

Beck looked at her, his wide eyes saying the same thing she was thinking. The first things Marcy listed were not small items in Violet's opinion. In fact they were giant red flags that should be relationship enders all on their own.

But since she'd overlooked all of Thomas's faults until it was literally impossible to do anything but acknowledge them, there was no way she was passing judgment of any kind here.

"Roxy needs surgery and I don't think it's a

good idea to wait. She is already dehydrated and weak."

"And she needs a muzzle because she hurts so much." Marcy rubbed the doodle's ears, but Roxy didn't react. She just looked at Marcy with sad eyes that nearly broke Violet's heart.

Marcy looked at her girl, pinched her eyes closed, sucked in a sob, then straightened her shoulders. When she opened her eyes, they were brimming with tears, but there was a resolution in them.

"I can't afford more than two thousand dollars." She pushed a tear away from her cheek. "I know how much these operations cost." Marcy's bottom lip quivered. "She's my best friend. I don't want to put her down, but I can't afford…"

Marcy sobbed, but she didn't drop her shoulders or look away from Violet. "If it is more than that, I need to talk about what we can do to end her suffering."

It was more, significantly more. But Roxy was well loved. Marcy was kicking her no-good boyfriend to the curb. Violet couldn't let her lose her best friend too.

"It's fifteen hundred. For all the medicine and surgery and everything." She saw Beck's head snap in her direction, but she didn't look at him.

"I can do that. I can do that. Oh. We will be eating peanut butter and jelly and mac and cheese for months. But it will be worth it." Macy kissed Roxy's head. "When?"

"Beck will get her prepped now. She will stay with us through tonight and maybe all of tomorrow. I know it is hard, but you should go home. Get some sleep."

"And hire a locksmith," Beck offered. "Seriously, if you kick Trevor out, hire one to make sure he can't get back in."

"No need." Marcy kissed Roxy one more time. "I can do that myself. My mother made sure I knew how. I'll stop at the hardware store as soon as they open."

"Good for her." Beck went the cabinet and grabbed the clippers they used to shave the fur where they'd put the IV port.

Yes, it was. The only recommendation Violet's mother ever gave her was to stay away from men. Advice she'd adhered to after Thomas's stunt. But that wasn't the right answer either.

Life was full of love and loss, joy and grief. The main thing you had to do was get out before you got your heart stomped on.

Her eyes found Beck. He wouldn't stomp on her heart. *Would he?*

"I'm going to get myself prepped." She headed for the door before she let her brain wander any further down that path. Beck had made it clear. He didn't plan to marry. Hell, he even had a rule about it.

And she wanted a life partner. Wanted the boring photo.

But not yet. She wasn't ready to give up the fun she was having with Beck.

There's still an expiration date.

That thought was going to get harder to ignore. She knew that, but that was future Violet's problem. She'd deal with the loss when it was time. For now she didn't want to let him go.

"Should we take an over under on the number of socks in Roxy's belly?" Vi stepped up to the operating table where Beck had prepped the large dog for her surgery.

"We both saw the X-ray. It's at least three and maybe as many as five." Beck never underestimated a big dog's ability to scarf down a whole host of things it shouldn't. "We'd be betting the same thing."

"True. We are on the same wavelength on that."

"Same wavelength." Beck chuckled. "My dad used to say that to my mom."

"Ah."

The soft sound sent a ripple of want through him. Same wavelength. For a second it almost felt like his dad was over his shoulder cheering him on. He really would have loved Vi.

"First incision completed." Violet looked to him, her dark eyes catching his.

"All her vitals are stable."

"Right. Then now we get to the moment of truth." She made the next incision and let out a grunt. One sock, then another, and another and another. Four total. And a small ball. "That—" Violet held up the hacky sack ball "—started all of this."

"If Marcy wasn't going to break up with Trevor for the other reasons already, that would do it." Beck shook his head. "I swear the bar is so low for men sometimes."

"Nice to hear a man say that." Vi glared at the hacky sack ball one more time, then tossed it aside. "A little weird, but nice."

Beck kept his eyes on the monitors in front of him. He didn't think it was weird, but he'd heard more than one woman he dated mention that his views were a pleasant surprise.

People deserved partners who were present. Who saw what they needed and acted. It wasn't magic and the fact that a not-as-small-as-he'd-like subset of men felt that they were entitled to more even though they couldn't manage the minimum was frustrating as hell.

"You are pretty perfect, ya know." Vi was smiling behind her mask as she met his gaze.

Perfect. Heat bloomed on his skin, and his heart raced. Perfect.

Before he could work through the funnel of emotions bearing down on him, the monitor's alarms started going off.

"Oxygen is dropping," Beck called as he adjusted the oxygen flow for Roxy. "Heart rate decreasing. She's reacting to the anesthesia."

"Come on, Roxy," Vi muttered as she worked to keep the dog alive. "Your mommy needs you to snuggle, and beg for food. Actual food. Not socks."

Vi was panting as she finished the surgery as quickly as possible. Some dogs reacted to anesthesia. If they could close her up and wean her from the drugs, she might start responding.

"Closed, increase O2 and start to pull her off the anesthesia." Vi watched the numbers as Beck made the requested changes.

Roxy's heart rate started to come up but not as fast as he'd like to see.

Beck held his breath and looked at Vi. She was clearly thinking the same thing.

"Up the oxygen one more time."

He did as she instructed and let out a sigh as the dog finally started to respond.

"Yes. Yes." Violet leaned over and pressed a hug to him. "We did it."

"We did."

CHAPTER TWELVE

HE COULDN'T STOP tapping the wheel as he drove them to Mitch's studio. The date he'd planned for last week was finally happening. The surprise was the best he'd ever planned.

"You all right? You're nervously tapping that wheel." Vi laid a hand on his knee. "I'm going to love whatever you have planned."

"Yeah, you are." Beck grinned at her. She deserved so much. The woman looked after the needs of so many people. And animals. She wasn't taking any money for training the intermediate team. And Roxy had needed another surgery two days after they'd pulled the socks and ball from her intestine. Vi had covered that too.

Though Dr. Brown had given her a strong warning that the choice was kind, but it could bankrupt her if she wasn't careful.

Vi had told him that she'd accepted long ago that she'd rather just break even than turn away a loving owner. Plus she'd told Marcy it was a donor. It wasn't like everyone was going to assume it was her.

Bangor was a city with more than thirty thousand residents, but Beck suspected more than one pet owner knew it was Vi covering the expenses. If it leaked out, Dr. Brown might have a point.

"So sure of yourself." Violet leaned over and kissed his cheek. "That is quite the turn on, Beck."

"I'm not sure you really need any help getting turned on." Beck took one hand off the wheel and slowly traced his way up her thigh. They'd been inseparable since returning from Miami. She'd slept at his place nearly every day and gotten ready for their late shifts together.

It was homey. Maybe a little too homey, but he was doing his best to ignore the tiny voice in his head shouting that she was looking for a husband.

The studio was in the back of a rundown little area. Mitch, the stained-glass artist he'd found, had said it was so if there was ever a fire or explosion, unlikely but not impossible with the heat he was working with, it would limit the damage.

"Where are we?" Vi leaned forward.

"I know it doesn't look like much but trust me." He'd stopped out here a few weeks ago and initially wondered if he'd wandered into the wrong place. But the inside of the studio was brilliant.

"I trust you." She unbuckled her seat belt as soon as the car was stopped. "I kind of thought we might be hiking given the requirements for my feet here." She looked around. "But I don't see any trails."

"The reasons for the shoes will be clear in just a moment, I promise."

"Beck!" Mitch called as he stepped out of his studio. The aged hippy had long white hair pulled into low ponytail. He was wearing a heavy apron and his cheeks were rosy.

Stepping up to them, Mitch offered a hand to Beck, then turned to Violet. "And you must be the artist."

"Umm." Vi looked from Mitch to Beck, then shook her head. "I'm no artist."

"Sure you are. You're human. That means you're an artist." Mitch clapped and motioned for them to follow him.

"Trust me," Beck repeated. When he'd finally gotten Mitch to return his phone call, the retired art teacher had waxed poetically about art and creativity for nearly ten minutes before launching into the training program for stained glass.

He'd told Beck the reason was that anyone lacking the patience required for stained glass was going to hang up before the ten-minute mark. A unique strategy but if it worked for the man, who was he to judge?

"Oh my God." Violet put her hand over her mouth as she stepped into the art studio.

Stained glass hung in all the back windows— Mitch had called those his bad stock—not sellable. Beck had no idea what imperfections Mitch saw. All he could see was beauty.

"We are having a stained-glass lesson?" Violet looked at him, her eyes filled with tears.

"Vi. It's okay. We don't have to. Why are you crying?" This was supposed to make her happy. What had he done wrong?

"I don't know." She bit her lip and looked at the floor as she pushed the tears away. "I'm not sad. Just...overwhelmed. This is the absolute sweetest thing anyone has ever done for me."

"Yes. Yes. It is very sweet. I do not normally take students. So are we learning art today?" Mitch clapped his hands and Violet snapped to attention.

"Yes. We are learning art today." She did a little happy dance and moved over to where Mitch was standing.

Why the tears? All he'd wanted was to make her happy. And it had, but for a split second her tears were sad not happy. He was nearly sure of it.

"Oh. I get to pick a design. How fun." That was the bright happy Vi voice he was used to.

He looked at her and Mitch and his heart jumped.

He loved her.

Beck put a hand on his throat. How had that happened?

He wanted to mentally shake himself. It had happened because Vi was Vi. She was funny, kind, exciting, smart and gorgeous. She was the easiest person in the world to fall in love with.

Settling down with her would be easy. He could do that, right? Maybe it was years earlier than he'd anticipated ever marrying. But Vi, Vi was worth it.

"Are you coming?" She looked at him. "I'm making the giant key chain."

"First time for that one." Mitch laughed and gave Beck a thumbs-up.

When he'd gone over the premade designs they'd have for options tonight, Beck had instantly pulled the giant key chain. Mitch had tried to talk him out of it. He only got five presets—and according to Mitch he'd created that design one night when he'd smoked a little too much marijuana. He left it in the selection pile as a silly reminder to himself.

Beck had known the instant he'd seen it that Vi would pick it. Pick it, love it, hang it…

Where would she hang it? Her apartment didn't have many windows. His place. Well, his place had plenty of natural light.

"Beck?" She raised her hands again showing the key chain. "Come pick or I will pick for you and we don't need two key chains."

She giggled as she turned back toward Mitch. *We.*

Such a simple little word. One she'd probably

used without any thought behind it. But he…he wanted to be part of that we.

As long as he could keep from entering the boring life. Surely he and Vi and could win against what his father said was an inevitability of a settled life.

The key chain she'd set in place wasn't very pretty. Even though she knew it would shine in the sun, the imperfections were easy to see. And Violet didn't care at all.

She'd made it. Her first piece of stained glass. This was the best present.

Violet swallowed the unexpected pain that raised. This was supposed to be a fun outing. It *was* a fun outing. But the second she'd figured out what he planned, her soul had screamed with joy before her heart felt like it was bursting.

She'd pulled herself together.

Then Mitch had chuckled when she'd chosen the key chain. Apparently, Beck had picked it specifically with her in mind. A throwaway line about collecting them on her travels—a line she barely remembered saying—had resulted in this beautiful monstrosity before her.

No one else had ever listened so freely to her. Ever internalized the things she said.

She looked over at him, bent over his design. Her heart swelled and her soul cried out that he was meant to be hers. She loved him. When it happened, how, why. None of it mattered. The truth was simple and terribly complicated. She loved Beck Forester.

That wasn't supposed to happen in a fling. Though technically his rule had been no marriage not no falling in love.

Not falling in love was an unstated rule. One she'd broken—splintered.

Beck wasn't interested in long-term. And she understood. He was twenty-six. Sure other twenty-six-year-olds were celebrating five- or six-year anniversaries and having their second or more children. But it was still young when you looked at it.

He wasn't ready for that life. Might never be ready. And that was okay.

Violet had no interest in children. At least not human ones. She enjoyed snuggling her friends' little ones. And enjoyed passing them back when they needed a diaper change or had spit up. Her mothering ways were all focused on fur babies.

That part of life wasn't for her...but she was ready for commitment. Ready to take the next steps with someone.

And the man I love isn't.

"What do you think?" Beck held up the mushroom with a rabbit hiding under it. His looked about like hers did.

Violet held hers up. "We did pretty awesome for one lesson."

"Maybe after we've been doing it for a year." Beck chuckled.

"Are we going to do this for a year?" It was like her words were hanging in the heated air. Spinning out of control as they raced toward him.

"I—" Her mind was devoid of all things. She looked for Mitch. Maybe there was some question she could ask about stained glass. Something, anything.

But the aged art instructor had taken himself out for a smoke break. Of course.

"Do you want us to do this for a year?" Beck raised an eyebrow, his dimples looking so damn lovely even in the heat of the workstations.

"What are you asking?" This couldn't be happening. It wasn't happening.

"We never set a deadline on the fling. Never said it had to end at a certain time. It could go on."

"For a year?" Hope pressed against her chest. She wasn't the same person she'd been when they scheduled this fake dating.

Wasn't the same person who'd gotten on the flight to Miami. No, that wasn't fair. It was the "Monster Mash" song. Winning the bet had awakened something in her. Reignited the spark she hadn't felt in so long.

"Or longer." Beck winked.

Tears pricked her eyes again. But this time it was joy racing through her.

"Or longer." Vi leaned across the bench and kissed him.

CHAPTER THIRTEEN

"I THINK MY face paint is scaring Larry the parrot. The bird keeps cursing at me anytime I pass his cage. And not his usual stuff either. Really foul innuendoes." Lacey glared back at the cage where the parrot was staying for the next four nights.

Dr. Brown didn't typically let patients board for nonemergency issues, but Larry had a habit of tricking anyone his owner, Mandy asked—or bribed—to look after the twenty-year-old African Grey.

His first owner, a creep Violet had—lucky for him—never met, had left the bird to its own devices and it had learned a lifetime of destructive habits. Mandy had dated Mr. No One Mentions His Name and taken Larry with her when they'd split less than four months later. The bird loved Mandy. He tolerated Dr. Brown.

The rest of the people in this world were things for him to squawk foul language at, scratch or bite.

"I don't think it is your Halloween makeup.

And even if it is, that just means Larry is a bad judge of character. You are the cutest orange cat." It was truly impressive. Lacey had painted her face orange and then added the white lines you usually saw on orange tabby cats. The woman looked like a life-size orange cat.

Thankfully Lacey wasn't up to the mischief that orange kitties seemed incapable of not finding.

"I am pretty proud of this one." Lacey smiled. "But mostly I am proud that you showed up in costume tonight." She clapped as she pointed to the orange scrub top, red scrub bottoms that she'd rolled up to reveal knee high orange socks. "That Velma from Scooby Doo costume is perfect!"

It wasn't exactly a Velma costume, but given her role as an emergency vet, the full costume wasn't hugely practical.

"Thanks." She'd pulled it together after Beck had suggested they have a couple's costume. He had all the items for Fred and she had the items for Velma. It was a quick find but it was fun standing in the mirror at his place in the joint costume.

He was handing out candy until his shift started, and she was more than a little excited to see Lacey's reaction to his matching costume. They were dating; everyone knew and no one seemed surprised.

It was going well. And they were certainly staying busy. When they weren't training at the agility gym, Beck had something up his sleeve. In the week since they'd visited Mitch's stained-glass studio, they'd gone hiking—twice—and spent their free night on a ghost hunt. It was fun…and exhausting.

Beck always had an idea. A game plan. Something fun to do. She loved Bangor; it was a beautiful city. But it wasn't what one would call a hub of nightlife. Yet, Beck seemed to have an endless supply of ideas. He was talking about skydiving when the winter was over, and a weekend trip to Canada as soon as her passport was updated.

Like he is worried I'll get bored. Or he will.

That was a useless thought. They were dating. Having fun together and getting to know each other. He'd mentioned still being together in a year. A year was not a fling. A year was commitment.

"Fred's here!" Beck strode through the back entrance, in blue scrub pants, a white top, with an orange bandanna around his neck.

"You guys match." Lacey did a little happy dance. "Oh. That is so cute."

"And you make the perfect orange cat, except you are far too brilliant." Beck winked.

Lacey stuck her tongue out at him. "Just because all of them seem to share the same brain cell is no reason to pick on them." She folded her arms but failed to keep a straight face. "At least they are cute."

"They do have that going for them." Beck nodded and headed to the sink to wash up.

A squawk followed by a stream of unpleasant language echoed around them.

"Good evening to you too, Larry."

A bell rang and Lacey darted to the reception desk.

Violet wandered over to Beck, leaned against the sink beside him and kissed his cheek. "You were right, even with the scrubs, everyone knows we are Fred and Velma."

He brushed his lips past hers, the touch barely there. "It is the spirit of the night, not the costume. Plus anyone who isn't frantic when they come in here tonight will pay us no attention when they see Lacey. Seriously, she is a master with the makeup."

It wasn't a competition, but he was right. If it was, their receptionist was taking all the prizes.

"How many kids did you pass out candy to?" She'd been shocked by how much candy he'd procured for the evening, particularly since her shift started as trick or treat began, and his started before it was over.

"About thirty. Not bad for an hour."

"I used to love trick or treating. My friends and I would take pillowcases and do our best to fill them with all sorts of treats. I bet I walked two to three miles every Halloween. We did it well into our teen years when we were the biggest kids out there." Those were some of her best childhood memories.

Her parents had never cared to come with her. They bought a costume at a local box store or told her to find something in her closet. She'd gone as a black cat at least four years in a row.

"I never got to go." Beck cleared his throat as he moved away from the counter.

"What?" He'd spent nearly twenty minutes in the grocery store trying to pick out candy. He'd gone back and forth between a few bags, before she'd just dumped both in their cart and told him they could always put extra out at the clinic. It would disappear faster than one could say abracadabra.

"Halloween is one of the most dangerous nights of the year for a kid." Beck shrugged.

That was probably true. It was nighttime and kids were running around, many like her, unsupervised. But the stat had to be skewed too. Because it was the one night where a large majority of children were all doing the same thing.

"On average children are twice as likely to be hit by a car and killed on Halloween than any other day of the year. Many of the costumes are cheap and fire hazards or contain dangerous levels of toxins. And of course jack-o'-lanterns start an average of nine hundred house fires a year."

Violet blinked, not quite sure what to do with that sobering information.

"I heard that every year. Every year, when I asked for a costume or begged to go trick or treating. I told them once that millions of children trick or treat each year and while the loss of any life was tragic the odds were in my favor." Beck frowned as he looked down at his shoes, clearly not sure what to do with himself.

"What did they say when you pointed it out?" She wished he'd said this when they were buying candy. Wished he'd pointed it out when talking about costumes. Wished they were anywhere other than work with a patient checking in. He needed to be held. Needed to get out whatever anger or frustration was brewing under that statement.

"They were excellent statisticians. They worked out the odds and decided it was too much. They loved me so much they weren't willing to risk it."

"Beck."

"They loved me. Treasured me. I know that. I know I sound bratty for even caring about trick or treating."

"You don't." He'd been loved and smothered. Two things could be true at once.

"I need to triage the patient. Hopefully, it's nothing serious."

He left before she could say anything else. But what else was there to say?

A lot. Just not here at the clinic.

* * *

"I looked away for a split second and she grabbed the candy from my hand. I got it back but she ate some chocolate and…" Belle Sanchez was running her hands over the black Lab mix that she'd brought home from the shelter less than four days ago. "Lucky, I am so sorry."

Belle hiccupped as the dog wagged its tail.

"Take a deep breath for me." Beck wasn't overly worried about Lucky. Chocolate toxicity was a threat, but Lucky weighed over forty pounds. Serious toxicity usually set in after they ate more than half an ounce per pound of their body weight. In Lucky's situation that meant twenty ounces, which was several full-size candy bars. It was always possible there were underlying conditions or that the dog might have an unknown allergy but part of a snack size candy bar was not overly a concern as long as Lucky continued to the act like she was perfectly fine.

Lucky licked Belle's face and put her paws on her shoulders as her owner continued to cry.

"Breathe for me, Belle. Lucky is fine."

"Chocolate toxicity can take up to twelve hours to show up." Belle bit her lip as she looked at her watch. "It might just be too soon."

The internet provided a lot of good information. Information he was glad the general population had access too. However, particularly for people with anxious personalities, it could come with a host of worries.

He pressed the button on the side of the cabinet that would alert Vi that he needed her in the room right now. Unfortunately, there wasn't a way to alert her that the issue was the pet parent not the pet.

Belle was spinning, worrying that she'd done something wrong. And he suspected that she'd read every horrid thing that might happen with chocolate toxicity.

His mom had googled the stats for every activity before he was allowed to participate. Football—concussion risk. That one was fair. And as more data was coming, he even understood her worries. Swimming—drowning risk. Except you were infinitely more likely to drown if you were scared of the water or didn't know how to swim.

Trick or treating…

That one still upset him. He'd missed out on such a common experience of childhood. And the truth was the activity was quite safe if the parents or guardians paid attention.

"Lucky had very little chocolate. You did a good job." Beck kept his voice soft, but firm. She'd done exactly right. Gotten the chocolate from the dog and started monitoring.

"What seems to be the problem?" Vi walked in, so cute in her scrub Velma outfit.

He'd never done a couple's costume. Never

wanted to. But when she'd mentioned finding something for the evening it had popped out. It would have been better for it to pop out at least a day before their Halloween shift, but they'd made it work.

"Lucky gobbled chocolate." Belle sobbed as she buried her head in the dog's coat.

"Not exactly accurate." Beck handed Vi the notes he'd written up. "Lucky had a part, a small part, of a snack size candy bar. Belle acted fast and got it away from him, but she is worried about chocolate toxicity."

"The internet—"

"Is full of scary things about dogs and chocolate." Vi interrupted, stepping up to the exam table. "I am not saying it isn't real—it very much is. But it takes a lot of chocolate for a dog this size to succumb to it. Even if you had a teacup Chihuahua, we wouldn't panic unless it ate the whole bite sized piece and was showing symptoms."

"But it can take time." Belle was repeating exactly what she'd told him.

Maybe Vi could relieve her worries.

Though once his mom had started an anxiety spiral it sometimes took days for her to come out of it.

"It can. But Lucky is acting perfectly fine." Violet held up a hand. "Let me explain what you should be looking for…"

Vi began to outline the symptoms of chocolate toxicity, asking Belle if Lucky was exhibiting any of them. With each negative response, Belle seemed to take a deeper breath.

"So you think she will be okay?"

"I do." Violet nodded. "She is very lucky to have you. It was a good name choice."

"The shelter chose it. I didn't think it was kind to change a name she was already responding too." Belle ran her hand down Lucky's back.

Dogs didn't really care what their humans called them, provided they were rewarded with love, food, play and the occasional treat. He'd let more than one pet parent know they didn't have to keep the name a shelter or previous owner gave their pet. But they absolutely could too. There was not a right or wrong answer with a name.

"I always wanted a dog, but my parents were very against animals in the house." Belle kissed the top of Lucky's head. "I had a dog, Misty, that my parents made me leave in the backyard."

Beck saw Violet shudder. Dogs could and should enjoy being outside. But, unless they were guardian livestock animals, then they needed to have a place in the home too.

"One night when it was snowing so hard, I snuck Misty into my room. It was so cold…and when my mom found her the next morning, well, Misty went to live with someone else then."

"I am so sorry, Mandy." There was nothing else he could say. He wasn't surprised. A cold truth of working in veterinary medicine was learning that many people should never have pets.

But Mandy was not one of those people.

"I saw Lucky on the shelter site and knew she was mine. I know that sounds weird but the picture…she was looking into the camera and I just had to go get her, and then I have her less than a week and I feed her chocolate."

"No." Vi shook her head. "You did *not* feed her chocolate. She took it from your hand and you immediately reacted and then got her seen by a vet. You did everything right, Mandy."

Mandy looked from Vi to Beck. He nodded. "She is right. That is why she has fancy degree hanging behind the receptionist's desk."

"You really think she's going to be all right?" Mandy looked at Lucky like she was trying to peer into her gut to find the exact amount of the offending candy.

"I do, but we'll give you a list of things to look for over the next twelve hours. If you see her reacting in any of the ways outlined, then you bring her back and we'll go from there. But you were a good dog mom today." Vi stepped up to Mandy. "Do you want a hug?"

Mandy stepped into Vi's arms. Not enjoying being left out of the affection, Lucky let out a bark and tilted her head as she surveyed the women.

"Thank you. I was just so worried." Mandy wiped a tear from her cheek as she stepped back.

"One thing that might help is getting her into training. There are basic dog training classes offered at the Happy Feet Gym or you can learn a lot through online videos." Beck had used online videos for Toaster's initial trainings. "The biggest things you want her to have without fail is 'leave it,' so she doesn't take food or other items that are bad for her, 'stay,' so she doesn't move from the place you need her and 'drop it'...in case she doesn't follow number one as well as possible."

"But—" Vi pointed a finger "—we don't go down rabbit hole videos of terrible things that might happen to our puppy. We live in the present. Not worrying about a future that is out of our control. Right?"

"Right." Mandy nodded, but he could see that she wasn't 100 percent behind following that advice. The woman was going to google and he doubted this was the first time they'd see Lucky in the ER for a minor thing.

"Beck will get you all set up with the signs and symptoms and if you have concerns, call the clinic." Violet offered her one more smile before stepping out of the room.

He gave Mandy the information packets on training, what to look for with chocolate toxicity. Lucky wagged her tail, happy to be headed home as they walked through the door.

As he stepped into the back room, Vi looked up. "Do you think I calmed her down?"

"Yes. For how long? I don't know." Beck blew out a breath and looked at the closed door. His mother had heard from countless doctors that Beck was fine. That playing sports was good for him. That independence was something to cultivate.

But she'd been too scared to risk losing the son she'd waited so long for.

Now he did it all.

"I can fix so many things, even mild to severe chocolate toxicity. But I can't fix a worried pet parent who is just trying to do their best."

There wasn't anyone else back here, and there were no patients actively waiting on them. Beck pulled her to him, kissing the top of her head.

"We do the best we can, Vi."

She looked up at him, her dark gaze smoky in the matching costume to his.

"Think there will be any candy left to dig into when we get home?"

Home. She'd referred to his place as home. He smiled, enjoying the simple phrase. "I think so. Someone made me buy far too much candy."

CHAPTER FOURTEEN

BEAR FLOPPED ON the floor next to Toaster, who opened an eye but didn't bother to get up. As soon as Beck mentioned getting her run in, the border collie mix would focus on nothing else, but at least for the moment she was willing to just relax.

"I feel the exact same way, guys." Violet took off her shoes and hung her coat up on the rack Beck had by the door. All she wanted tonight was to order in and stream some mindless television show.

It wasn't that the Halloween shift had been bad. It had simply been a steady stream. All of the animals they'd seen tonight were either already going home with their owners or headed there after short stays at the clinic. That was a good thing, but it didn't mean her battery wasn't drained after moving from one crisis to another.

"So, I was thinking that tomorrow we might go to the Rock Shop. They are having a discussion on natural history." Beck bounced into the room, holding two mugs of decaf coffee. "Or we could rent some bikes and go—"

"Or we could stay home and rest." Violet interrupted, as she took her cup of coffee from his hands. "Thank you."

She held the mug up to her lips enjoying the smell and the warmth in her hands. She had a strict rule about caffeine after her night shifts. If there was any hope of her maintaining some kind of regular sleep schedule, she couldn't have it just after her shift.

No matter how much she craved it.

"We could take a day off." Beck leaned forward his lips brushing hers.

The touch sent fire through her, but his words froze her heart. "Beck, we do not have to always be doing something." She had a better understanding of why he felt the need to try new things after what he said about his mother not letting him try anything.

Including trick or treating. Outside of Christmas that was the best holiday as a kid. The one night a year you were allowed to take candy from strangers.

Being told that was too risky would leave a mark on anyone. Even make them thrilled to jump on a plane and go to a wedding with a colleague as a fake date.

Spontaneity and an openness to try new things

were good traits. But just like his parents, it was possible to swing too far the other way.

"Sure, we don't have to, but we don't want to become boring immediately." He took a sip of his coffee and snapped his fingers.

Toaster popped to attention and moved toward the back door.

"While I take her for her agility run, why don't you find something for us to binge on our boring night." Beck moved to follow Toaster.

"Watching television does not have to be boring," Violet called out as she heard the back door open.

Boring. That was his focus. Or rather the thing he was trying to avoid at all costs in life.

She looked at the television, picked up the remote then set it down. Toaster and Beck would be on his makeshift course outside burning off her energy for at least thirty minutes.

She wanted another look at the boring picture—as he called it. Maybe she'd missed something when she'd looked at it the first time. Maybe there was a clearer meaning to why it bothered him so much.

An answer to why he couldn't just relax in their relationship.

Beck took one more breath of fresh air as Toaster rounded the corner of the A-Frame. His girl had run for a solid thirty minutes. And he'd used every one of those seconds to beat himself up.

They'd had a long night. Two dogs had gotten loose and tangled in chicken coop wire a neighbor had left out, resulting in deep cuts to one's hind legs and the other's abdomen. A dog had come in after eating a bag of candy—and unlike Lucky they'd had to induce vomiting and were keeping the poor guy overnight to watch for chocolate toxicity. And just before their shift ended, a cat with smoke inhalation from a barn fire had been rushed in by a farmer, whose night had gone from fun Halloween games to nightmare.

The animals were all going to recover. Not a thing he got to say about every shift. But the hug they'd shared after talking to Mandy was the last moment of free time they'd gotten.

And he was complaining about spending the rest of the day sleeping, watching mindless television and cuddling with the woman he loved.

Get a grip, Beck!

Toaster panted at his side, waiting for the command to run the backyard course again or to go in.

"Let's go see what Vi picked out." Beck snapped two fingers and Toaster turned and walked to the back door.

She stopped at the water bowl while he continued to the living room. The screen was dark. The couch empty.

Bear was lying on his bed.

"Where is your mom, Bear?"

The pittie opened his eyes, let out a yawn but gave no further indication to where Vi might be hiding.

Stepping into the hallway he froze. Light poured out from under the crack in his parents' study. "Vi?"

"I'm in the study," she called back.

He knew that. But had hoped she might pop out and explain why she was spending any time in there when she could be curled on the couch with a pittie. Instead, he was going to have to go into the one room in the house he disliked.

Once upon a time he'd loved the study. Loved sitting at his parents' feet while they worked and talked. They'd chatted continuously. About important things, nothings, and everything in between.

When his father died, the room had quieted and when his mother had to move into a full-time care facility, it had silenced forever.

"What are you doing in here?"

"Looking at photos." Vi held up a box with prints from his parents' years together.

"Some of these are great. You should put them in frames. Or maybe we could take a scrapbooking class. This one should be in a frame!" She smiled up at him as she held up a photo of his mom and dad in the kitchen. His mom holding a beer while his father cooked.

The irony of the photo taken in the late eighties with the gender roles swapped was not lost on him. But it certainly wasn't frame worthy. It was just a picture of how they'd been.

His father had joked that he'd had to learn to cook because his mother had no ability to do it and no willingness to learn. She'd always laughed at that and told his dad there was no reason to learn when she'd married a master.

"Seriously, Beck." Violet reached for another picture, but he picked up the box before she could.

"These are nothing. They are just day-to-day pics. Nothing exciting."

"That isn't true." Vi crossed her arms, shaking her head. "These are exciting in their own way."

"Exciting." Beck put the box on his dad's desk and grabbed her hand. "I'll show you exciting." He pulled her to the hallway where he'd framed an image of his father on top of a mountain.

"And this one—" he pointed to a hiking picture "—this is exciting."

Turning, he pointed to another image, this one of his father on an archaeological dig. One of the few archaeological digs he'd taken part in after he'd married Beck's mother. Those trips dwindled away, and the rest was boring history. "This was one of Dad's last digs. Do you know how old he was?"

Vi squeezed his hand. "Beck."

"Seriously, Vi. How old do you think he is here."

"Thirty-five?"

"Nope. Twenty-nine. Twenty-nine years old. Do you know how many digs he could have gone on? How many trips he just didn't even try for? And why?"

"Because he loved your mother." Her face fell as she said the words.

"No." That was the rub of it. He didn't think their love had anything to do with it. It was the marriage certificate. The piece of paper that made them one in the eyes of the government that had changed them. "It was marriage."

Vi opened her mouth, then shut it. She crossed her arms, rocking back, her eyes glued to the floor in front of her.

Away from me.

The space between them was less than three feet but crossing it seemed impossible.

"My parents argued every single day. They screamed at each other. Threw things. Blamed me for their lot in life."

"Vi—"

Her gaze rooted to the floor. "I don't have a single photo of them happy. My dad burned the wedding photos after an argument. My mother ripped up the pictures of their early years after another."

She wiped at a tear on her cheek. "Maybe that's why I think a cooking photo or a garden party where two people seem content with each other in a crowd of people is so exciting."

Beck swallowed, hoping it might free the words caught in his throat. This was a crossroad. A junction. A point that shifted everything.

"Sorry I barged in here. I was—" Vi finally looked up, but instead of looking at him, she let her gaze wander around the room. "I don't actually know what I was thinking."

"Movie time?" The suggestion sounded a little hollow on his lips, but Vi smiled. Not a full smile but a smile.

"Sure. We should order some food too. I'm hungry and neither of us are master cooks." She hit his hip with hers, but the motion he'd come to enjoy so much over the last couple of weeks didn't have the oomph behind it.

"Did you cut your hair?" Nikki tilted her head as she looked at Violet. The owner of one of the local hair shops was always fishing for her to come in and let her play with her color. Nikki was currently sporting a bright red bob with junky blond highlights. It wasn't Violet's cup of tea, but if it made her happy then that was what mattered.

"Nope. I have an appointment with my regular gal in a week or so just to trim the dead ends." Violet blew a loose strand of hair out of her eyes. She was going to pull it back into a bun shortly. She seemed to start some shifts with the idea that today was the day she just left it down. And halfway through, or sometimes minutes into her shift, she just lost it and yanked it into a ponytail or messy bun.

"Well, I think you'd rock a blond, or maybe even some purple. Mix it up."

Violet made a noncommittal sound, hoping Nikki would launch into the pet-related reason she was here.

"Something about you is different." Nikki looked at Beck, then pointed at her. "Don't you think something is different?"

Beck grinned. He knew exactly what was different with her. Knew that she was waking up satisfied in his bed. Coming out of the shell she'd wrapped herself in when Thomas left her at the altar. It was a rebirth, and she was enjoying every minute.

Well, nearly every minute.

Their argument two nights ago was still stuck in her head. Argument, fight, misunderstanding... all of those words seemed too much of a descriptor.

And yet somehow not enough.

She'd give almost anything to have a love like his parents. They glowed in the photos. People she'd never get to meet, who'd created the sweetest man she'd ever known.

And he didn't want what they'd had. Scorned it even.

"You are sure you didn't cut your hair?" Nikki

looked at her. "You just have that something fresh vibe going on."

"I think I would know if I cut it," Violet laughed. "But we aren't here to talk about my hair." She took in the large male tabby very unhappy to be in the carrier Nikki had him in.

Nikki looked at her giant orange cat and smiled. "He'll calm down as soon as I get him out." She unzipped the carrier top, lifted the giant up and sat him on her shoulder.

"We just sent an angry parrot home, and I would have loved to snap a picture of Larry on a shoulder and then have Frank on yours." Beck let out a chuckle as the orange tabby ran his head along Nikki's.

"Yeah, my husband started this when he was a kitten. It was cute when he weighed five pounds. Even when he weighed ten…but at seventeen it can be a bit much." Nikki ran a hand along Frank's back, and the cat let out a satisfied rumble.

"You told Beck he was here because of a string missing from your sewing basket."

"I have looked all over for it." Nikki playfully glared at Frank. "And given his history…"

Frank had consumed about six inches of fishing line two years ago. It had wrapped around the back of his tongue as it moved through his intestines requiring emergency surgery and several nights at the clinic.

Cats were typically better than dogs at not eating inedible items, except for string. There was something about the movement of it that made their predator instincts flare.

Violet wasn't exactly sure what caused it, but she'd removed as much string from cats in her career as she had socks from dogs.

"But you aren't sure he ate it." Beck added as he pulled up the X-ray. "There is nothing there, but that doesn't necessarily mean anything."

She looked at the X-ray. If Frank had eaten the string a few hours ago, there was little the images could provide and it was too soon to see a blockage.

"I think our best bet is to administer a purgative." That would clear Frank's stomach and hopefully pull up any string he'd eaten.

Beck left to get the medication.

"While Beck is gone, let's just go over what will happen."

"You're going to make him throw up." Nikki shrugged and Frank let out a meow at the shift in his perch. "This is not his first rodeo on these. Honestly that is the cheapest option, though he is going to be pissed."

Violet smiled as she ran a hand over Frank's ears. The massive boy rumbled and pushed his head against her hand. "You aren't going to like me for much longer. I should get the attention while I can. Or maybe I should make Beck do it."

"Maybe you should." Nikki giggled as she

pulled Frank off her shoulders and cradled the cat in her arms. If Frank minded the change in his position, he did not show it.

"So, while we wait, let's get back to you. It's not your hair and you aren't wearing makeup." Nikki squinted at her, then her mouth widened. "You're dating someone."

"I am." Heat poured over her cheeks. Violet knew Nikki from the clinic, and while Bangor was one of the largest cities in Maine, it still felt like a small town sometimes. Maybe if she knew something was different she'd move on.

"I'm very happy." Violet plastered a smile on, hoping Beck would be back with the medication shortly. She liked Nikki as a client. The woman loved Frank, which was what was most important. But she didn't know her well enough to talk about her relationship.

"Ooh." Nikki clapped. "Maybe we will be seeing you in a white dress soon?"

"Maybe," Violet offered as the door opened. She'd learned when she first arrived in Bangor that if she didn't want to carry on the conversation, *maybe* was the best way to curtail the conversation.

A *yes* or *no* seemed to bring on advice. Or questions to try to get her to dive in deeper. A *maybe* was wishy-washy enough that the person she was talking to could reasonably assume she agreed with them, even if she didn't.

Beck handed her the medicine, and there was the ghost of question in his eyes.

"Was there a problem finding this?" She looked at the box, checking the expiration date and the dosage. Beck would have done that too, but it was protocol for the techs and the vets to each check.

He looked at Frank and then Nikki, but not at her. "No. I just had to make sure we had enough for him. He is a bit of a big guy." Beck pulled on the long heavy gloves and took a deep breath. Frank was a sweet boy, but no cat liked having a syringe shoved down his throat.

Before Frank could make sense of what happened, Beck had him pinned. The yowls started immediately.

"I did warn you that you were going to be mad at me." Violet quickly slid the medicine behind his tongue, pushed it out then closed his mouth, forcing Frank to swallow.

If the feline could speak, the curses might even make Larry the parrot blush.

Beck let go as soon as the medicine was in and Frank took off. He was under the bench, glaring at all of them.

"So now we wait thirty minutes and see if it works, right?" Nikki crossed her arms as she looked at the angry orange creature she'd brought in.

"Like you said, it's not his first rodeo. So you know the routine. If he starts to do anything, I want you to push this button and I will come to make sure it goes as smoothly as possible." Cats were notoriously difficult patients. They rarely showed symptoms until it was almost too late and unlike dogs, induced vomiting did not have a high success rate.

"I will. And if you ever want to talk about the hunk you are planning to meet at the altar, you let me know. And keep me in mind when you need wedding updos. I give group rates." Nikki sat on the bench, pulling her legs up quickly as Frank swatted at them.

They were certainly personae non gratae with the usually friendly feline.

"Okay." Violet waved as she headed back through the door. As Beck closed it, she held up her hands. "I haven't been planning or scheming a way to get you to the altar. I know we aren't going there. I just didn't want to discuss it and I said maybe and Nikki assumed and—" Her words ran out as he shrugged.

"It's not a big deal, Vi." He kissed her cheek. "You want to get married someday and I don't plan to. But we are having fun now." He winked, then moved off to the patient in the next room.

Violet buried her hands in her scrubs pocket, her fingernails cutting into her palms as she balled her hands. She was trying to explain and he'd shrugged it off. But not because he was worried she was trying to force the issue he'd said was a nonstarter.

He'd indicated he saw them together. Indicated they had a future.

She wasn't overly concerned about a wedding license. Marriage wasn't the only way to commit to someone. But he saw an end date for them. A final point. Not today or even this year, but he expected their chapter to close.

Pinching her eyes closed she willed the tears away. There was a time for them. And there were going to be a lot of them—soon. But not here.

Not yet.

CHAPTER FIFTEEN

BECK RACED ALONG the weave poles, cringing as Toaster missed the third one again. How was that possible? Weave poles were her favorite obstacle.

The agility competition was this weekend. He knew Violet was trying to pretend that she didn't care about whether their team placed. Knew she was actively avoiding any thoughts of running into Thomas.

Which was 100 percent going to happen since the man seemed hell-bent on seeking them out at his stepbrother's wedding. He could only imagine what it was going to be like when they were on his "turf" so to speak.

"Beck." Vi's voice was firm as it hit him from the other side of the gym.

So she'd seen the mess up—again.

He was hoping she was focused on Tim or Lacey. She probably had been, but the woman seemed to pick up everything in the agility gym. It was like her radar pinged every time perfection slipped away.

"I know. I know." He held up his hand. "Toaster faulted on the weave poles. We'll run it again." He gave the command for Toaster to follow him back to the start of the obstacle.

She let out a soft whine but followed the command.

Before he could get her started, Vi raced over. "Stop."

"What?" He crossed his arms, then immediately uncrossed them. "I mean what?"

He was touchy. Had been touchy since Nikki mentioned doing Vi's hair for her wedding.

No, it was Vi's explanation after. Her insistence that she didn't plan on marrying him. Nikki loved to play the matchmaker. Loved to do wedding hair and makeup. It was her salon's specialty, and she was always stumping for business. He hadn't thought that much of it—until Vi jumped to explain.

She wasn't planning on meeting him at the altar. It was what he'd asked for. What he wanted.

He had no reason to be bothered. But he couldn't seem to shake off the anxious thoughts.

She was pulling away. It wasn't much. A few less touches. An extra night stayed at her place.

With each day it was like they were slipping further away from each other. But neither was willing to acknowledge it. Maybe they were scared to.

Violet tilted her head, looking from him to

Toaster. Then she sat on the ground and motioned for Toaster to come sit in her lap. It was one of Bear's favorite games. Despite the pittie's sixty-pound weight, Bear truly believed he was a lap-dog.

Now Toaster felt the same was true for her.

"You are doing great, girl." Violet rubbed her face in Toaster's hair. Beck's dog wagged her tail so hard her whole body was moving.

"Not sure that is quite true. We've faulted each time on the run through the weave poles tonight." Beck crossed his arms as he stared at the obstacle. Usually it was a no-brainer for Toaster. Was it just that they hadn't practiced this one much that she was faltering?

Vi kissed Toaster's nose, then looked up at him. "It's not Toaster that's faulting, it's you."

Beck blinked, not sure what to say to that. "I'm running the course the same way I always do, Vi. Right down the center, snapping my fingers for her and calling out commands. We do this every night either here or in the backyard. Literally." There was nothing different now than there had been yesterday.

"You're stressed. And she is picking up on that." Violet swallowed and looked away. "If you want to talk about what is bugging you, we can do that."

"Not here we can't."

Vi nodded, and he saw her bite her lip. "So it

is us." She kissed Toaster on the head one more time, then pushed herself up off the ground.

"Vi—" He hadn't meant to hurt her. That was never his goal. He loved her. Loved her so much.

But Thomas had been right. She wanted a husband. Deserved a husband. A quiet steady love. And he was holding her back.

So let her go.

The words blasted through his brain, but his heart refused to recognize them. How could you love someone and know you weren't there forever?

She could be.

His heart had refused to listen to his brain since day one with Vi.

"Violet. I have a question about helping Tuna with her banks. She is pushing off the center and dangerously close to the fault line."

She looked over to Lisa and Tuna, putting on her trainer face. "We'll talk after practice." Vi looked at him, her smile breaking just a little before she jogged off to help Lisa.

"It's late and we have a long day tomorrow. What if we just put off the conversation until we wake up?"

Beck's offer was too good to pass up. Even though Vi knew they should hash it out now.

Coward.

She'd opened a chasm last week when she'd

looked through his parents' things. And it had widened after Nikki's wedding jokes.

They were both walking on eggshells around the other. Both knowing what might be coming and neither willing to pull at the thread that was growing impossible to ignore.

"You hungry?"

"No." Violet dropped her bags by his front door. Her stomach was rolling too much to think of putting much sustenance in it. "You?"

"Not for food." Beck raised his eyebrows in the silly manner he had. It was a running joke they had. One they hadn't used since she'd gone through his parents' stuff. So many of their little fun things had ended after that.

Because it was the end of our fling.

That was the moment. The true moment this became a relationship. One doomed to fail.

Fiona had told her once when they were in college and she was dating some frat guy that she swore was fun but not forever that you either dated to marry or to break up.

"Beck." She pulled him close—clinging to him as she traced kisses down his neck. This wasn't what they should be doing, but Vi didn't care.

She needed another night with him. One more time with the man she loved. She could say goodbye tomorrow.

His arm wrapped around her waist, arching her toward him. "Vi."

Her name, whispered on his lips undid her.

"Take me to bed, Beck. Now."

Tomorrow. Tomorrow they'd talk. Tomorrow she'd figure out what the next steps were. Tomorrow she'd face heartbreak head-on.

But tonight was hers and Beck's. All theirs.

Beck rolled over and wasn't surprised to find the bed empty. Pulling a hand over his face, he stared at the ceiling. They'd spent the night cocooned in each other.

Each touch weighted with a meaning he didn't want to look at too closely in the morning light. They had today off. He'd planned to see if she wanted to go hiking again, or maybe to the market to see the Christmas decorations. The market had put up the trees and snowmen as soon as the trick-or-treaters had headed to bed.

Thanksgiving might be in between Halloween and Christmas, but no one was paying that holiday any attention.

Now though.

He heard Bear bark and a little worry slipped from him. Part of Beck had worried that she might disappear on him. Last night was the most intense night of his life, other than the first night he'd loved her.

They were together. Each anticipating the other's needs, the other's wants. But the last time.

The last time they'd gone slow. Taking their time, memorizing everything about the other.

Saying goodbye with their bodies before they said it out loud.

She wanted marriage. She deserved marriage. She deserved someone who knew they wanted that life.

He got out of bed and looked around his room. Her stuff was gone. Beck slid his hand across the bedside table where her book and reading lamp had been sitting last night. Her clothes were no longer on the oversize chair in the corner.

He stood, knowing what he'd find in the bathroom and needing to see it anyway. Her makeup, toothbrush and hairbrush were no longer scattered on the extra sink. It was like she'd packed up all the pieces she'd left.

She was going to be the first to leave this time.

There were two options. Take his time getting ready, prolong what they'd already prolonged last night. Or rush through it and embrace the heartbreak waiting for him in the kitchen or living room. Neither option appealed to him, but hurrying ended the suspense fastest.

The aroma of coffee filled the hall on his way to the kitchen, and his mouth watered as he heard the bacon sizzling. If her things weren't gone from his room, he might assume this was just another day for them.

"Good morning, Violet." The words were thick as he took her in.

Her dark hair in a low ponytail; black leggings with a green sweater pulled over top. She had on long gray socks that if she put on boots could roll over the top. Vi looked ready to go the Christmas market.

But there was a look in her eyes. A hint of the conversation they'd put off last night.

Pulling the bacon from the skillet, she put it on a plate, then moved to the table and sat down while he fixed his coffee.

"Thanks for breakfast." Beck grabbed a slice of toast from a plate she must have set out before the bacon and took a bite. He didn't expect a fight, but getting a meal and sitting down wasn't what he'd prepped for either.

"What was the issue last night?" Vi sipped her coffee, her dark gaze holding his. No accusation, just a question.

"You want to get married." He rolled his thumb on the edge of the table. "I don't."

"Have I said I want to get married?" Vi tilted her head, tapping her fingers against her plate.

"Not directly."

"So no." Vi took a deep breath. "Why do you think I want to meet anyone at the altar so badly? My one failed trip was a fairly large disaster."

"Thomas—"

Vi scooted back in her chair at the mention of

her ex, crossing her arms. "Our relationship has nothing to do with Thomas."

"It does, actually. It has everything to do with him. He is the reason you were so shut up here in Bangor for years. He is the reason you didn't want to go alone to Miami. He is the reason you invited me. He is the reason…"

"Stop." Vi shook her head. "You being terrified of commitment has nothing to do with my ex. Yes, he was a catalyst but—"

"I saw you at Fiona's wedding, Vi." He wasn't afraid of commitment. One day, he'd probably settle down. Be the boring husband. He just wasn't ready to hang up the fun quite yet. "I watched you participate in the bouquet dance. I saw how disappointed you were when the bouquet went to someone else. Yes, you covered it quickly but it was there." He'd seen it. Real disappointment.

"I was disappointed." Vi shrugged. "I like to win and that was a fun bouquet. Fiona made it out of recycled brochures if you remember. Not exactly the usual kind of thing you get during a bouquet toss."

Beck blinked. Had he read that situation wrong? Built that moment into something more? "You want a relationship."

Vi nodded. "I thought that was what we had, but—"

She blew out a breath and looked out the window. He followed her gaze. His stained glass still hung there. Hers was gone. Another piece of herself she'd removed from his place while he slept.

"But you are right. We want different things. I want someone committed to me. Someone who sees a future with me. Someone who wants a quiet, steady love that is comfortable in the boring parts of life."

"So marriage."

"You are the only one using that term. I don't care about a ring or a piece of paper." Vi stood up, put both hands on her stomach. "I want someone who sees a future with me. Not someone who is terrified that by loving me, they will lose themselves. Your parents found themselves in love."

He opened his mouth, but she held up a hand.

"You are diminishing them by calling it boring. It was right for them." She grabbed her plate and mug and walked over to the sink.

"I think you've been looking for a reason I might leave since we decided to date. I mean all of your stuff is already packed up. Worried that I might try to keep something like Thomas did? You don't even know that I care about you enough to make sure you have everything you wanted."

Violet looked to the window where her stained-glass key chain had hung when they went to bed this morning. "I think we're agreed that we aren't a good match. We still have to work together and we are going to Boston soon. We are adults, this was a fling, so…"

She looked at him and he had no words.

Say something!

No. This is for the best.

Tell her you love her.

We want different things right now.

Do something.

His heart and his brain warred with each other as she pushed away from the counter, but he couldn't manage to work anything out.

He let her leave. Didn't run after her when the front door shut. This was the right thing.

So why did it feel like his soul left with her?

CHAPTER SIXTEEN

THREE DAYS. It had been three days since he'd let Vi walk out of this home. Toaster nuzzled his hand, and he rubbed the top of her head.

"I miss her too. Not that I haven't seen her every day." They'd worked two shifts together and done the final touches on the agility team yesterday. They'd professionally ignored each other.

That was the best description for the coolness between them. It wasn't just the light touches and stolen kisses in slow moments that he missed. It was the silly banter, the quick platonic hugs after tough cases. The simple conversations.

Even Lacey had mentioned that the temperature seemed to drop ten degrees every time they were in the room together. But what else was he supposed to do?

In two days the team would leave for Boston. Except instead of riding with him and Toaster down to the facility, Vi was carpooling with Nancy. The gym owner had Oliver in a few single competitions and had gladly offered Vi a ride so she didn't have to drive by herself.

He suspected Nancy would spend the entire time chatting about training manuals, techniques and all things agility. Given that they were rooming together, Nancy was going to have a lot of time to pick Vi's brain. Clearly, Vi would do *anything* rather than voluntarily spend time around him...

Beck got up and moved through the kitchen. Since she'd left, staying still had become a real issue. Which was funny because he always joked that he never liked to be still. He was always planning things. Going on adventures. Seeking new things.

Running from his parents' life—if Vi was to be believed.

"She isn't right. I'm not running."

Toaster tilted her head and let out a bark. She was sweet company but not the best conversationalist.

Looking at the closed door to his parents' study, he crossed his arms. He could march in there right now, look at that bucket of old photos and prove her wrong.

"I don't need to."

Again, Toaster tilted her head.

"Sorry, girl. Just talking to myself." Beck started toward the door. He'd look at the one picture. The boring pic. It was all he ever needed to remind himself that he wasn't going to follow their path.

Stepping into the room, he took a deep breath and looked at the picture. His dad was looking at his mom. It was the exact same as it had been for as long as he could remember.

Her in a bright dress, the sun hitting just right on her face. His father looking at her. The rest of the world gone. Nothing about it had changed.

But…

Beck ran his hand over the glass. His father's face was brilliant. He raced toward the picture he kept of his father in the living room. Him on top of a mountain.

Beck had climbed that mountain right after college graduation. Stood on the top and had another hiker snap his picture re-creating his father's photo. He kept meaning to hang it next to his dad's.

Now, looking at the two pictures of his father, it was easy to see which one radiated happiness. And it wasn't the one of him alone on a summit.

No.

He moved to the hallway photos, each was the same, his dad looked fine, happy even. But not content.

Reaching for his phone, he pulled up the photo Callie sent him after the first time he brought Vi to the gym. She'd told him congrats—and that she was retiring from trying to find him a date.

He stared at the picture.

People had always told him how much he looked like his mother. He had his father's height, but his facial features and hair were all his mother. But in this image, looking at Violet like there was no one else in his world, he was his father's spitting image.

He loved her. And rather than telling Violet that he couldn't see a life without her in it—instead of inviting her on the adventures he wanted to take—he'd let her walk away.

How did one make up for that?

How did he even begin to show her how sorry he was?

The idea formed quickly. He wasn't sure it was possible but for Vi—for Vi he'd do anything.

The image of them standing on the agility course, love pouring from him long before he'd even realized it, bolstered him as he started trying to track down the one person who might be willing to help him.

Soft music poured through the speakers in Nancy's car. Violet had expected to spend the entire trip to Boston answering agility questions. Instead, Nancy had asked how she was doing then asked if Violet minded classical music.

The music choice wasn't her favorite, but Nancy was kind enough to offer her a ride. And she hadn't peppered her with any questions about Beck.

Violet bit her lip as his name echoed in her mind. Five days into forever without him. And it hurt more than she could have ever imagined.

And she'd been left at the altar.

Following the demise of her engagement, she'd been hurt. Embarrassed. Mad at herself for not recognizing the signs that Thomas was all wrong for her.

But the soul crushing emptiness she felt now hadn't appeared.

"Did I ever tell you why I got into agility?" Nancy's question offered a nice respite.

"No." Violet was sure Nancy knew she'd never told her. She was trying to distract her.

The gym owner might be more than a little too uptight about the gym, and her rules for trainers were actively keeping them away—though she'd loosened them after Vi had pointed out some of the issue. But she'd offered the ride to Boston quietly without pressure.

"What made you get into the sport?" Vi smiled and turned her attention to Nancy.

"My ex-husband." Nancy laughed. A true belly laugh that made the crow's-feet around the older woman's eyes deepen.

"Your ex-husband was into the sport?" Violet had seen all sorts of things when she worked in Miami. One couple had even gone to court over who maintained custody of the dog.

"No. He hated dogs."

"Good riddance then." Violet chuckled. Thomas was an ass, but the man genuinely liked animals. It was his only redeeming quality.

"Exactly." Nancy nodded. "I got a border collie the second we separated. He told me he'd file for divorce if I didn't get rid of the dog."

"Men." Vi rolled her eyes.

"I told him that was not the threat he thought it was." Nancy quickly looked back at Oliver.

"Good for you."

"Yes. Lilly was my baby, but as a first-time dog owner border collies are…" Nancy put her finger on her chin.

"A lot." Violet finished the thought. "There is a reason I never recommend that breed to new pet parents. They are bred to work."

"Yes. Lilly was a lot. I started driving to an agility gym two hours away." Nancy started tapping her fingers on the steering wheel. "It was fun to learn. Lilly and I had the best time."

"It's a great sport for humans and dogs."

"I fell in love with a trainer." Nancy let out a sigh. "You remind me of him sometimes. So professional. So knowledgeable but focused on the dogs and people not the trophies. But in other ways you are me. I can see it so easily. Maybe it's a benefit of age or something."

Vi didn't know what to say.

"We had a wild affair. The best six months of my life." Nancy blew out a breath.

Now she wished she'd said something. She looked at her lap, not sure how to end this conversation. The feelings she was not burying well on her own were now ready to spill over in the car with Nancy.

"He was my great love and I let him go. I was so worried that I might lose the independence I gained from my ex. I put all my fears from the relationship on him—something he didn't deserve. When I realized I loved him, I pulled away instead of running toward him."

"Nancy—"

"I opened the gym four years after the last time I saw him. He passed less than two weeks after our final fight, a car accident."

"I'm so sorry."

Nancy didn't look at her as she kept spilling her heartbreak. "I'd give up anything for those two weeks. Anything for more time. My ex got to win in the end because I was too stubborn to start over."

The older woman took a deep breath. "I don't know what happened with you and Beck. And it is the definition of not my business. But you are not the same person you were before him. I don't know why and I don't need to. And maybe he did something unforgivable."

"He didn't."

Nancy bit her lip, like she was weighing saying something else.

"The past is there to learn from, but those who hurt us can jade things they have no business jading." Nancy looked at the radio and shook her head. "No more classical. Time for some hard rock."

The heavy beats blasted through the car, and there was no way to have a conversation. Mentally she sent a simple thank you to Nancy.

Violet had packed up her things—shocked at the number of items she'd actually moved into Beck's place. She would not have said they were living together, but her car's trunk was full of stuff that she'd transitioned to his space without even thinking.

And then there was the stained glass. She packed that first. Not that Beck knew it.

Everything else at his place was technically replaceable. But not that key chain. She'd grabbed that first in case he woke while she was busy.

Because I didn't trust him.

She'd let her fear take control. A fear she'd developed from Thomas and thrown over Beck.

They'd needed to have a conversation. She'd needed to ask if he saw a future with her. Needed to work through his issues fearing marriage. All of that was needed.

But she'd packed up first. Guaranteed the outcome of the conversation. For someone who craved loyalty and steadiness, she'd walked first.

"How close are we to the facility?" Violet called over the rock music.

"Just under an hour. Plenty of time to work up a speech." She winked at her, then started singing along to the ballad blasting from her radio.

It's here. Standing by concessions will leave in five if you are not here.

Beck read Dove's text and took off at a sprint. Luckily Toaster was so well trained she kept up with him perfectly.

The concessions came into sight and Dove was standing there looking nervously around, holding a package wrapped in brown paper.

He held out a hand. "Is that the tablecloth? I can't tell you how much I appreciate this, Dove. I know this must be awkward for you."

She passed it over and nodded. "I didn't realize that it was— Look, just tell her to keep it off social media, okay? He won't notice it's gone if no one draws attention to it. I don't know why he even took it to be honest. It's not really his style of decor."

Beck was pretty sure he knew why, but he wasn't going to say so in front of Dove after she'd done him this favor.

"Thanks again. It will mean a lot to Vi."

"Sure. You don't need to tell her how you got

it though. Just keep my name out of it, okay? I don't need any problems."

"Of course."

As she spotted her doppelgänger weaving through the crowds looking for Beck, Dove looked startled and quickly melted away into the background before he could say any more. Delighted to see her, Beck made his way toward Violet and the world disappeared as she wrapped her arms around him.

"I'm sorry, Beck." She whispered the words in his ear and he was stunned.

"You have nothing to apologize for. You were right. I was so terrified of becoming a homebody, but I looked at the picture of my parents again. You were right. They were alive when they were together. Truly alive. They didn't need more."

"But you do. And that's okay." Violet wrapped her hand through his.

"I want more adventures, but I want you beside me while I take them. While we take them. I love you, Violet. I love you so much. I should have told you so many times. But mostly I should have told you when you were so worried about my reaction to people talking marriage. That issue is mine not yours, and I put it on you." Beck ran his hand down her back, so grateful to just have her here.

"I love you too. And you weren't the only one

letting your personal stuff get in the way. I was looking for any sign I might get left. That you might not want what I wanted. I let fear rule me and I took the first chance to leave so didn't get hurt. That wasn't fair." Violet's hand cupped his cheek. "I love you."

"I love you too, Vi. And I've got something for you. Something you've been missing for a long time." Her eyes fell on the package in his hands and she opened her mouth, then shook her head. "No. Is that…?"

He passed her the package and watched her remove the brown wrapping. "I will admit that I got this because I was hoping to use it to win you back."

Vi laughed. "You don't have to win me back, but—" Her fingers gently touched the cloth and tears sprang to her eyes. "How did you…?"

"Oh, don't you worry about that. I have my ways."

"Oh thank you, Beck. Thank you so much."

Beck's lips brushed hers, and Toaster let out a bark. "If I wouldn't be letting the team down, I would say we could get out of here." He pulled her even closer.

"I say we go beat Thomas's team, then spend the night making it up to each other. Maybe stay an extra night in Boston. The Holiday Market at

Snowport is already open, and I hear it is quite the place to be this time of year."

"That sounds like the perfect plan." Beck kissed her cheek. "The perfect plan indeed."

EPILOGUE

"WHAT DO YOU THINK?" Vi held up the secret project she'd been working on at Mitch's studio. The one that Beck was not allowed to peek at. The one that she wasn't 100 percent sure he'd like.

Beck put his hand over his mouth. To hide his horror?

"Vi." Tears clouded his eyes as he stared at the stained-glass window. A re-creation of his parents' favorite photo.

The "boring one," as Beck still referred to it. Though now he said it with a grin on his face.

"If you don't like it—"

"I love it."

"Oh good. Because if you hated it after it took me nearly a year to work out, I might have burst into tears right here." Vi chuckled as Beck stepped toward her.

They'd lived in his home for almost three years now. And she was certain he'd love this gift on the day she'd started it. But as the image took shape and she was framing it, part of her had feared the argument they'd had years ago regarding the photo might resurface.

A wild fear. Totally baseless.

"I do wish Mom and Dad had gotten to see it." He took the framed glass from her hands and put it up on the mantel next to the image of him and Vi skydiving last year on vacation in Florida.

"We are going to have to put it in an actual window. Don't suppose you know a class that will teach us how to install a full-size stained-glass window?" Beck reached for her, pulling her close.

"No, but I bet Mitch can help us figure it out." Violet leaned her head against his shoulder. The man who'd taught them stained-glass techniques was a jack-of-all-trades, and his home had many stained-glass windows in the panes.

"You really think they'd have liked it?" She'd never get to meet the lovely people that raised the man she loved more than anything. She hoped they liked the woman he'd chosen as a life partner.

"They'd have loved it." Beck kissed the top of her head. "Which brings me to another thing they'd have loved."

He turned and got down on one knee.

Vi pulled her hands over her mouth as tears filled her eyes. "Yes. Yes. A million times yes!"

"I haven't asked anything yet, Vi." Beck had tears in his eyes too as he looked up at her.

She pursed her lips, even though he couldn't

see them behind her hands to keep her mouth shut long enough for him to ask the question.

"Will you marry me, Vi?"

Before she could say anything, Toaster and Bear bounded into the room, saw Beck on the floor and took full advantage. The dogs knocked him over, and he let out a grunt as the two covered him with kisses.

Vi couldn't have stopped the belly laughs if she wanted to. Tears were pouring down her face; happiness filled the whole scene.

She'd meant what she'd told him years ago. She didn't need a ring or a certificate. Marriage and a life partner were one and the same to her as long as they had each other.

This was the life she'd craved. A happy home with a partner who adored her.

"Can you stop laughing long enough to answer?" Beck called from the literal dog pile.

"Yes." She giggled a little more, then said, "Heel." Toaster was immediately at her side. Bear looked at her, nuzzled Beck one more time, then sashayed over to her side.

Beck stood and she held out her hand. "I love you, Vi. I love you so much. In the exciting times. The boring times. And every single moment in between."

* * * * *

*If you enjoyed this story, check
out these other great reads from
Juliette Hyland*

**One-Night Baby with Her Best Friend
Dating His Irresistible Rival
Her Secret Baby Confession
A Puppy on the 34th Ward**

All available now!